QUESTIONS O[N]
PRACTICAL CO[OKERY]

Victor Ceserani MBE, MBA, FHCIMA

Formerly Head of
The School of Hotel Keeping and Catering,
Ealing College of Higher Education

Ronald Kinton BEd (Hons), FHCIMA

Formerly of
Garnett College, College of Education
for Teachers in Further and Higher Education

To accompany *Practical Cookery* sixth edition

Edward Arnold

© Victor Ceserani and Ronald Kinton 1987

First published in Great Britain 1976 by
Edward Arnold (Publishers) Ltd, 41 Bedford Square, London WC1B 3DQ.

Edward Arnold (Australia) Pty Ltd, 80 Waverley Road, Caulfield East, Victoria 3145, Australia.

Edward Arnold, 3 East Read Street, Baltimore, Maryland 21202, USA.

Second edition 1981
This edition 1987

British Library Cataloguing in Publication Data

Ceserani, Victor
    Questions on practical cookery. — 3rd ed.
    1. Cookery — Problems, exercises, etc.
    I. Title   II. Kinton, Ronald
    641.5′076   TX652.7

    ISBN 0–7131–7664–4

Set in Linotron Plantin with Univers
Northern Phototypesetting Company, Bolton
Printed and bound in Great Britain
by Richard Clay Ltd., Bungay, Suffolk

Contents

Introduction

The aim of this workbook is to assist students of cookery in their revision by providing questions drawn mainly from the sixth edition of *Practical Cookery*. Students may work from the book on their own to test the effectiveness of their study of *Practical Cookery*, and their own general knowledge of the subject. The questions should be answered from memory, from the students' own deductions or by reference to *Practical Cookery*. It is the authors' opinion that revision by systematic use of this book throughout the course will result in a better knowledge of cookery.

Many multiple choice questions are included and the book will be particularly useful for students taking City & Guilds of London Catering examinations 705 and 706/1/2/3, as well as BTEC Certificate, Diploma, Higher Certificate and Higher Diploma Courses, and the membership examinations of the Hotel, Catering and Institutional Management Association.

At the top of each page of questions are the numbers of the pages in *Practical Cookery* where the answers may be found. Answers to multiple choice, mixed, humorous and illustrated questions can be found at the back of the book and questions which are not answered in *Practical Cookery* are indicated by an asterisk.

1
Knives

pages 1–3

1 State 10 safety rules to be observed when using knives.

1	6
2	7
3	8
4	9
5	10

2 Name this equipment (continues over page).

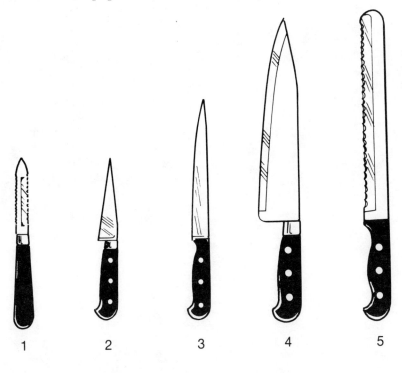

1   2   3   4   5

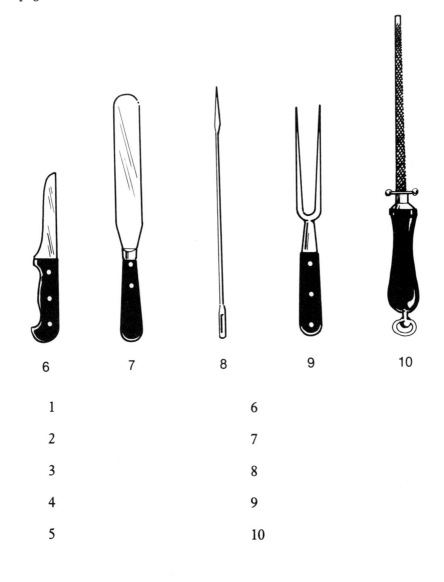

6   7   8   9   10

1   6

2   7

3   8

4   9

5   10

2
Useful Information

pages 6–8

1   What is the approximate metric equivalent of

1oz.............. ½lb.............. ¼pt............. ½in.............

4oz.............. ¾lb.............. ¾pt............. 2in..............

6oz.............. 1½lb.............. 1½pt.............

10oz.............. 2lb.............. 2pt..............

2   Give the centigrade oven temperatures for these regulo numbers

1 .... 7 ....

3 .... 9 ....

5 ....

3   What oven regulo number would you set for:

a) cool .... c) hot ....

b) moderate .. d) very hot....

4   Place the following commodities in order showing the one with lowest % of saturated fat first:

Beef dripping   Soft margarine
Butter   Sunflower seed oil
Ground nut oil   Olive oil

5   Fill in the blanks:

Natural yoghurt in place of cream.
. . . . in place of animal fat.
Instead of white flour use . . . .
Skimmed milk instead of . . . .
. . . . in place of full fat cheese.

pages 8–9

6   Food satisfies two requirements. What are they?

   a)   b)

7   State three points which provide enjoyment from eating food.

   a)   b)   c)

8   What is the purpose of cooking food?

9   What do you understand by the term pathogens?

3
Methods or Processes of Cookery

pages 12–14

1 List 12 methods or processes of cooking food.

1	5	9
2	6	10
3	7	11
4	8	12

2 Give a definition for boiling.

3 Give examples of foods cooked by boiling using:
a) fish
b) vegetables
c) meat
d) poultry

4 What particular consideration applies when boiling salted or pickled meats e.g. silverside of beef?

5 Approximately how long per ½ kg (1 lb) is allowed for boiling meat? (*Ans. p. 220*)

☐ 15 minutes   ☐ 25 minutes
☐ 20 minutes   ☐ 30 minutes

6 Vegetables grown above the ground are cooked in

☐ cold water   ☐ hot water
☐ warm water   ☐ boiling water

7 Vegetables such as turnips and cauliflower should be boiled gently otherwise they will

☐ taste strong   ☐ become mashed
☐ lose colour   ☐ lose flavour

8 Define poaching.

9 Poached foods are particularly suitable for whom?

10 Name three foods which may be cooked by poaching.

1

2

3

11 Specify two points which must apply when poaching food.

1

2

12 To which food, when poached, do the general rules not apply?

13 Why does the stewing of meat have nutritional advantages?

14 Which of the following meats is suitable for stewing?

☐ coarser types   ☐ prime joints
☐ tender cuts   ☐ young carcass

15 For which cookery process is each piece of equipment used?

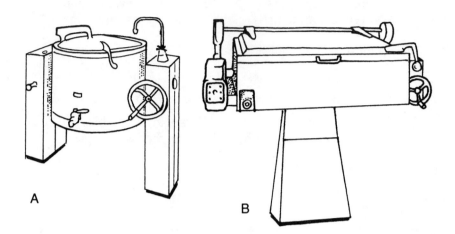

A

B

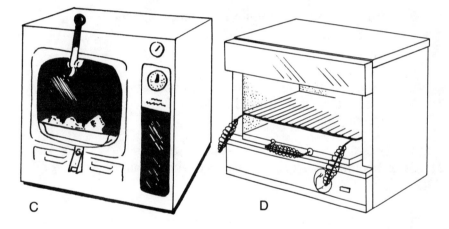

C

D

16 Give a definition for braising.

17 What is the main difference between braising and stewing?

18 Why is it necessary to use a pan with a tight fitting lid when braising?

☐ to protect the contents   ☐ to prevent evaporation
☐ to prevent colouration   ☐ to increase colouration

19 Why is meat sealed on all sides before braising?

20★ Meat may be marinaded before braising in a mixture of

☐ wine, vegetables and herbs   ☐ vinegar, vegetables and spices
☐ stock, vegetables and herbs   ☐ wine, herbs and spices

21 Name four vegetables which may be braised.

1   3

2   4

22 Briefly describe two different ways of steaming food.

1

2

23 Why are foods such as steamed puddings protected by foil or greaseproof paper?

24 State 3 points of safety to be observed when steaming foods.

1

2

3

25 Explain the difference between baking and roasting.

26 How does the heat of the oven cook a baked jacket potato?

27 Why are egg custards cooked in a bain-marie?

28 Toad in the hole is

    a) sausage in batter
    b) sausage roll
    c) a hot dog
    d) a ham roll

29 Describe the cleaning of tartlet moulds and cake tins.

30 What is meant by basting meat?

    ☐ inserting pieces of fat meat
    ☐ batting out with a cutlet bat
    ☐ spooning the cooking fat over the meat
    ☐ covering with a slice of fat

31 Define oven roasting.

32★ Why is basting necessary?

    ☐ to flavour the fat   ☐ to colour gravy
    ☐ to prevent drying   ☐ to increase evaporation

33 Beef when roasted should be well done: true/false.

34 Why is it essential to commence roasting in a pre-heated oven?

35 What is the difference between a conventional general purpose oven and a convection oven?

36 When roasting pork allow approximately

    ☐ 25 minutes per ½kg and 25 minutes over
    ☐ 20 minutes per ½ kg and 20 minutes over
    ☐ 15 minutes per ½kg and 15 mins over
    ☐ 10 minutes per ½kg and 10 minutes over

37 What are the approximate cooking times per ½kg (1 lb) for roasting

    Beef   Lamb

pages 25, 42, 30–31

38 Name two vegetables which may be roasted.

   1

   2

39 Describe the quality of meat, poultry and game which may be pot roasted.

40 State the advantages of pot roasting.

41 When pot roasting, what are the juices from the meat used for?

42 A fast method of cooking by radiated heat describes which method of cookery?

43 Which is the odd one out and why?

   ☐ cooking on a grill   ☐ cooking on a spit
   ☐ cooking under a salamander ☐ cooking between grill bars

44 How do you test the degree of cooked roast and grilled meat?

45 Describe three different ways of grilling food.

   1

   2

   3

46 Why are grill bars pre-heated and brushed with oil before use?

47 Name four terms, both English and French, which describe the degrees of grilling steaks.

English   *French*
1

2

3

4

48 Tomatoes and mushrooms are grilled under the . . . .?

49★ Why are certain foods grilled on trays?

☐ to improve the flavour   ☐ to cook them more slowly
☐ to prevent them falling   ☐ to colour them more evenly
    between grill bars

50 Define two methods of frying.

1

2

51 Explain the meaning of the term *sauté* when applied to cooking poultry or meat.

52 The word *ragoût* usually indicates:

☐ a lamb stew   ☐ a fish stew
☐ a beef stew   ☐ a game stew

53 Name four cooking mediums for deep frying.

1   2

3   4

54 Suggest two factors to consider when purchasing oil for deep frying.

1   2

55★ What is the price of olive oil?   Vegetable oil?

56 List eight points essential to ensure safe deep frying.

1   5

2   6

3   7

4   8

57 Why is it necessary to coat most foods which are to be deep fried?

58 Name three coatings which may be used to coat foods for deep frying.

1   2   3

59 Which of the following fruits are suitable for coating in batter and deep frying?
☐ bananas   ☐ strawberries
☐ apples   ☐ cherries
☐ pineapples   ☐ oranges

60 Foods cooked in batter and deep fried are called
in English   in French

61 Explain the principle of microwave cookery.

62 Can a microwave oven be used for defrosting food?

63 What is standing time?

64 Which substance must not be placed in a microwave oven?

☐ metal   ☐ plastic
☐ glass   ☐ paper

65 What major disadvantage has microwave cookery?

66 State three restricting factors to be considered when using a microwave oven for cooking food.

1   2   3

67 Why is a microwave oven so useful for reheating food?

68 With which method of cooking are these associated?

A   B   C

D   E   F

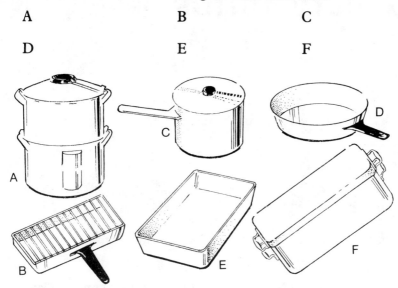

69 For which method of cooking do you need to know how to use these?

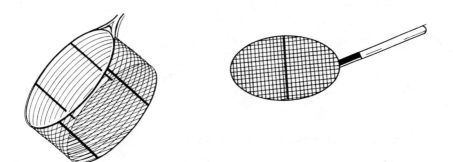

4
Culinary Terms

pages 45–46

1 What do you understand by the term offal?

2 What are giblets?

    ☐ poultry offal   ☐ type of bacteria
    ☐ fish fillets   ☐ a rice dish

3 What is French for 'in the style of' as used in menus?

4 'À la carte' and 'carte du jour' are two common terms; explain 'à la carte'.

5 What are bacteria?

    ☐ micro-organisms   ☐ small insects
    ☐ harmful rays   ☐ minute animals

6 Give three explanations of the term 'bain-marie'.

    1

    2

    3

7 What are bean sprouts?

8 Which is used during roasting?

    a) breading
    b) blanc
    c) basting
    d) ballottine

9 'Blanching' is a common culinary term with five meanings; define blanching in five ways.

1   4

2   5

3

10 What are crudités?

11 How do bouchées and vol-au-vents differ?

12 Match the following.

☐ brunoise	1	thin strips
☐ paysanne	2	½cm (¼″) dice
☐ macédoine	3	small dice
☐ julienne	4	thin rounds, triangles or squares

13 A canapé is a dish cover: true/false.

14 Carbohydrates consist of 3 groups; name all three:

1   2   3

15 What is the value of calcium to the diet?

☐ prevents skin disease   ☐ provides vitamin C
☐ builds bones and teeth   ☐ gives energy

16 What is the culinary meaning of clarification?

17 How is the term clarification used in the kitchen?

18 If you were asked for a chinois would you fetch a

☐ piping bag   ☐ conical strainer
☐ chef's hat   ☐ Chinese muslin

19 Clostridium perfringens are food poisoning bacteria; where are they found?

20 What do you understand by 'correcting' when related to a soup or a sauce?

21 Explain the difference between a darne and a tronçon.

22 Draw a simple diagram of a darne and a tronçon.

23 Deglaze means to serve on ice: true/false.

24 What is duxelle?

☐ chopped mushrooms and onions – cooked   ☐ chopped mushrooms and breadcrumbs – cooked

☐ chopped mushrooms and shallots – cooked   ☐ chopped mushrooms and minced meat – cooked

25 Give two examples of emulsions used in the kitchen.

26 How are the two emulsions in your answer to question 25 used?

27 Croûtons are served with velouté soups: true/false.

28 When are petits fours served?

29 Explain the difference between a blanquette and a fricassée.

30 Garam masala – what is it?

31 A liaison is for

a) tiering
b) turning
c) thickening
d) trussing

32 Give three different examples of the use of the term 'to glaze'.

1

2

3

33 What is the difference between mirepoix and macédoine?

34 Monosodium glutamate is used to increase flavour: true/false.

35 If you saw the term 'Native' on the menu what would it signify?

☐ a dish for locals   ☐ English oysters
☐ okra fingers   ☐ a speciality

36 What is the French term for food which has been egg and crumbed?

☐ piqué   ☐ bardé
☐ beignet   ☐ pané

37 What is a pulse?

☐ a dried pod vegetable   ☐ a vegetable soup
☐ a savoury rice   ☐ a dried fruit

38 The term 'refresh' is frequently used in cookery; what does it mean?

39 If you were working in the pastry what could you prove?

40 What is salmonella and where is it found?

41 What is staphylococcus and where is it found?

42 What is the culinary meaning of 'to sweat'?

pages 50, 328

43 In which order would you place these when crumbing food?

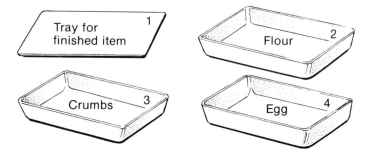

44 Name these cuts of vegetables

5
Stocks and Sauces

page 54

1 Explain what you understand by the term 'stock' when it relates to a liquid used in the kitchen.

2 Why is beef stock cooked for a longer time than fish stock?

3 Stock goes cloudy if it is

☐ boiled insufficiently   ☐ boiled too slowly
☐ boiled for too long   ☐ boiled too quickly

4 Why should only sound items be used for making stock?

5 State four points which indicate a good stock.

1   2

3   4

6 To achieve good quality stock it is necessary to:

1   2

3   4

7 Salt is omitted from stock because

☐ it prevents it from simmering   ☐ it makes it change colour
☐ it causes it to go sour   ☐ stock is used as a base for
                                    many dishes

8 Why is it necessary to skim stock?

9 What is the purpose of having brown and white beef stock in the kitchen?

10 What are the proportions of ingredients needed for stock (other than fish stock)?

11 Why is cold water added to stock just before boiling point is reached and why are the bones covered with cold and not hot water in the first place?

12 Describe the difference between producing a brown stock and a white stock.

13 What is the French term for brown beef stock?

☐ réchauffer ☐ estouffade
☐ ragoût ☐ espagnole

14 Fish stock should be cooked for

☐ 40 minutes ☐ 20 minutes
☐ 30 minutes ☐ 10 minutes

15★ Why is the time taken to cook fish stock important?

16 What are fish glaze and meat glaze?

17 Fish glaze and meat glaze are used to

☐ increase flavour ☐ improve the appearance
☐ save money and time ☐ improve texture

18 A sauce is a thickened liquid; name four ways in which the liquid can be thickened.

1   3

2   4

19 State four points which indicate a good quality sauce.

1   3

2   4

20 A roux is

☐ a thickening   ☐ an unusual vegetable
☐ a type of saucepan   ☐ a Russian sweet

21 Name 3 roux and 3 stocks and give an example of a suitable sauce for each.

1 roux   stock   sauce

2 roux   stock   sauce

3 roux   stock   sauce

22★ Why is less fat used when making a roux for brown sauce than when making a roux for white sauce?

23 Why should a boiling liquid never be added to a hot roux?

24 Name three ingredients which may be used to thicken jus lié.

1   2   3

25★ What do you understand by the word 'dilute'?

☐ to add liquid   ☐ to pass through a sieve
☐ to drain in a colander ☐ to put in a bain-marie

26★ Cost the ingredients for four litres of brown sauce.

27★ Cost the ingredients for four litres of white sauce.

28★ Cost the ingredients for four litres of fish stock.

29 How many portions will four litres of white onion sauce produce?

30 What two main items are needed to produce a velouté?

    1   2

31 Name four velouté sauces

    1   3

    2   4

32 What two items may be used to finish a velouté sauce?

    1   2

33 Caper sauce is served with;

    ☐ boiled mutton   ☐ boiled beef

    ☐ boiled bacon   ☐ boiled fish

34 A sauce .... is used in chicken vol-au-vent.

35 Name three sauces which are derivatives of sauce suprême.

    1   2   3

36 Which of the following is produced from espagnole sauce?

    ☐ caper sauce   ☐ demi-glace sauce

    ☐ ivory sauce   ☐ béarnaise sauce

37 How is a finished, refined brown sauce produced?

38 Name 6 sauces which are derived from a refined brown sauce.

    1   2   3

    4   5   6

39 Name the sauce which contains poached beef marrow.

40 Give the name of the dish with which the sauce in question 39 is used.

41 What is the name of the sauce which contains chopped shallots, sliced mushrooms, tomatoes, chopped parsley and tarragon?

42 Sauce diable is served with;

☐ grilled meat   ☐ roast meat
☐ cold meat   ☐ boiled meat

43 What is the main ingredient in sauce lyonnaise?

☐ mushrooms   ☐ gherkins
☐ shallots   ☐ onions

44 With what dish may sauce lyonnaise be served?

45 Chopped capers and chopped gherkins are used in

☐ sauce Robert   ☐ sauce piquante
☐ sauce poivrade   ☐ sauce charcutière

46 Côtelette d'agneau Réforme is a well-known dish; describe sauce Réforme.

47 Which of the following sauces contains duxelle?

☐ piquante   ☐ italienne
☐ Robert   ☐ charcutière

48★ What points indicate a high standard of roast gravy?

49 Name two dishes with which bread sauce is served.

1   2

50★ Why is apple sauce served with roast pork, duck and goose?

51 Cranberry sauce is served with roast turkey: true/false.

52 Match the following sauces with an appropriate dish.

☐ bread   1 fried lamb cutlets
☐ mint   2 roast chicken
☐ tomato   3 fried liver
☐ lyonnaise   4 roast lamb
☐ curry   5 fried fish
☐ reform   6 hard boiled eggs

53 Explain how beurre fondu, beurre manié, and beurre maître d'hôtel are used. (*Ans. for beurre manié p 58 in Practical Cookery*)

1

2

3

54 Name two different dishes with which hollandaise sauce may be served.

1   2

55 Why may hollandaise sauce curdle?

56 How can the curdling of hollandaise sauce be avoided?

57 How can curdled hollandaise sauce be rectified?

☐ by adding butter   ☐ by increasing the
☐ by whisking in a little hot water   temperature
                                          ☐ by more whisking

58 What is the difference between hollandaise and béarnaise sauces?

59 Why is a hard butter sauce served with grilled fish?

60 Give four reasons why mayonnaise may curdle.

1   3

2   4

61 Name two sauces which are thickened by using eggs.

1   2

62 Sauce verte could be served with

☐ cold turbot   ☐ cold ham
☐ cold beef   ☐ cold salmon

63 Which ingredients are needed to produce tartar sauce from mayonnaise sauce?

64 With what dish is horseradish sauce served?

☐ roast beef   ☐ roast veal
☐ roast lamb   ☐ roast venison

65 Mint sauce is traditionally served with

66★ Why is it very important to observe hygienic standards when using aspic jelly and chaudfroid sauce?

67★ What points of quality would indicate a high standard aspic jelly?

68 If stock is not used immediately what procedure should be followed? (*Ans. p 54*)

69 Sauces such as tomato, béchamel etc. form a skin on the surface; suggest how this can be prevented. (*Ans. p 59*).

6

Hors-d'oeuvre, Salads and Sandwiches

pages 78–82

1   What do you understand by the term 'hors-d'oeuvre'? (*Ans. p. 49*)

2   Into what two main categories may hors-d'oeuvre be divided?

   1   2

3   What accompaniments are served with oysters?

☐ brown bread and butter and lemon   ☐ melba toast and lemon

☐ white bread and butter and lemon   ☐ toast and lemon

4   From which fish is caviar obtained?

☐ shad   ☐ sturgeon

☐ salmon trout   ☐ salmon

5   What part of the fish is caviar?

☐ the roe   ☐ the young fish

☐ the marrow   ☐ the brain

6   How should smoked salmon be carved?

7   How should oysters be served?

☐ in a coupe   ☐ on a julienne of lettuce

☐ on a canapé   ☐ on crushed ice

8   How many oysters are usually served as a portion?

☐ four   ☐ six

☐ five   ☐ eight

9   What is the cost of oysters?   Caviar?
    Smoked salmon?

10 Pâté is usually cooked in a:

☐ timbale ☐ terrine
☐ sauteuse ☐ ravier

11 For grapefruit cocktail the grapefruit is cut into:

☐ halves ☐ segments
☐ quarters ☐ dice

12 State the points which indicate a well prepared grapefruit cocktail.

13 What have the following in common; ogen, charentais, honeydew and cantaloup?

14 Name four juices which can be served as a first course.

1 3

2 4

15 Suggest three ways of serving avocado pear.

1 2 3

16 The basic sauce for a shellfish cocktail is:

☐ mayonnaise ☐ hollandaise
☐ béchamel ☐ fish velouté

17 When buying crabs what points of quality should be considered?

18 When purchasing crabs why is it wise to buy them alive?

19 What sauce is usually served with dressed crab?

☐ sauce verte ☐ sauce tartare
☐ sauce mayonnaise ☐ sauce hollandaise

20 What part is discarded when preparing dressed crab?

☐ gills ☐ antennae
☐ claws ☐ legs

21 What is the culinary meaning of 'soused'?

☐ pickled in alcohol   ☐ cooked in vinegar
☐ kippered in smoke   ☐ saturated in oil

22 Name two kinds of fish which may be soused.

1   2

23 Suggest two ways of presenting a variety of hors-d'oeuvre.

1   2

24 Egg mayonnaise is presented in three ways on the menu; describe each, stating how much egg per portion would be used.

1

2

3

25★ Suggest six points to be considered when preparing a selection of hors-d'oeuvre.

1   4

2   5

3   6

26 Compile a list of eight items you would include in a selection of hors-d'oeuvre.

1   5

2   6

3   7

4   8

27 Produce a diagram showing how you would present a selection of hors-d'oeuvre on a plate.

28 Produce a diagram naming sixteen hors-d'oeuvre on a trolley.

29 Name five items which could be prepared à la grecque:

1   2   3

4   5

30 If a dish is termed à la portugaise which ingredient will be included?

☐ tunny   ☐ sweetcorn
☐ cucumber   ☐ tomato

31 Name eight food items which could be served at a cocktail party.

1   5

2   6

3   7

4   8

32 What does the word canapé indicate?

☐ specific garnish   ☐ cushion for food
☐ Russian cake   ☐ sliced sausage

33 Suggest six bouchée fillings.

1   2   3
4   5   6

29

34★ Add the appropriate name from:

Marmite   Cocotte   Ravier

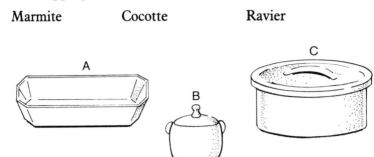

35 What is the difference between a simple salad and a mixed salad?

36 A dressing should always be offered with any salad: true/false.

37 Which is the most usual blend of oil and vinegar used when making vinaigrette?

Parts of oil	Parts of vinegar	
3	1	☐
4	1	☐
5	1	☐
6	1	☐

38 Name four suitable ingredients that may be added to vinaigrette in order to give variation.

1   3

2   4

39 What should one add to cream in order to make an acidulated cream dressing?

40 What are the four chief ingredients added to vinaigrette to make Thousand Island dressing?

1   3

2   4

41 What ingredients could you serve in a bowl of mixed salad?

42 What are the usual ingredients in a French salad?

43 A Florida salad consists of

☐ lettuce and grapes   ☐ lettuce and orange
☐ lettuce and grapefruit   ☐ lettuce and tomato

44 What dressing would you offer with a Florida salad?

45 Give the ingredients of a Japanese salad.

1   2   3

4   5   6

46 The chief ingredients of a Salad Niçoise are

☐ French beans, anchovies, potatoes, capers, olives, tomatoes
☐ French beans, peas, carrots, turnips, anchovies, olives
☐ French beans, tomatoes, potatoes, anchovies, olives, turnips
☐ French beans, lettuce, onions, pimentos, anchovies, olives

47★ What is the price of twelve English lettuce?

48★ What is the price of twelve Dutch lettuce?

49 These items would be used in salad – Mimosa, Waldorf or Niçoise?

Apple

Lettuce

Walnuts

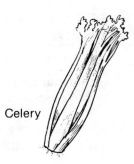
Celery

50 Suggest four different types of bread suitable for sandwiches.

1   2

3   4

51 Suggest an interesting variety of six sandwich fillings.

1   2   3

4   5   6

52 Suggest four examples of combination fillings for sandwiches.

1   2

3   4

53 Suggest five different seasonings that are suitable for varying the flavour of sandwiches.

1   2   3

4   5

54 Which of the following would you sprinkle on to a dish of sandwiches?

☐ chopped parsley   ☐ mustard and cress
☐ watercress   ☐ shredded lettuce

55 What is a toasted sandwich?

56 Give two examples of popular toasted sandwiches.

1   2

57 Two slices of hot buttered toast with a filling of lettuce, grilled bacon, sliced hard boiled egg, slice of chicken and mayonnaise is known as:

☐ savoury toasted sandwich   ☐ jumbo sandwich
☐ book-maker sandwich   ☐ club sandwich

58 What is the name given to an underdone minute steak between two slices of hot buttered toast?

59 What are the following?
double decker sandwich:

treble decker sandwich:

60 Give two examples for each
double decker: treble decker:

1   1

2   2

61 Give a brief description of an open sandwich.

62 Suggest four interesting varieties of open sandwich.

1   2

3   4

63 Open sandwiches are traditionally prepared with:

☐ fresh bread   ☐ toast

7
Soups

pages 105–110

1 Classify the soups.

2 Give an example for each class of soup.

3 How much soup is usually served per portion?

   ☐ 125 ml (5 fl oz)   ☐ 375 ml (15 fl oz)
   ☐ 250 ml (10 fl oz)   ☐ 500 ml (20 fl oz)

4 Suggest two ways of making a cream soup.

5 Specify the points which indicate a high standard consommé.

6 State the factors which are needed to produce a good quality consommé.

7 The colour of consommé should be:

   ☐ brown   ☐ pale amber
   ☐ amber   ☐ dark brown

8 Suggest six garnishes suitable for adding to consommé and state how you would write the name of each on the menu.

   1   2

   3   4

   5   6

9 What have consommé en tasse and consommé madrilène in common?

10 Briefly describe a petite marmite.

11 In what type of dish is a petite marmite traditionally served?

12 What are the accompaniments to petite marmite?

13 Which stock is used to produce Scotch broth?
　□ mutton　　　　　　　□ fish
　□ beef　　　　　　　　□ chicken

14 Name the cereal used to garnish Scotch broth.

15★ What characteristics has a broth of good quality?

16 A soup thickened by its main ingredient is called:
　□ velouté　　　　　　□ broth
　□ purée　　　　　　　□ potage

17 Which class of soup is garnished with croûtons?

18★ Describe the points which indicate good quality croûtons.

19 The main ingredient for Crème St Germain is:

20 The main ingredient of a purée soissonnaise is:
　□ lentils　　　　　　　□ haricot beans
　□ yellow split peas　　□ green split peas

21 The main ingredient of a purée parmentier is:
　□ potato　　　　　　　□ potato and peas
　□ peas　　　　　　　　□ lentils

22 The garnish for purée cressonnière is:

☐ rice   ☐ watercress
☐ carrot   ☐ chicken

23★ How is a good standard achieved when making a purée soup?

24 Name the two soups used to produce a Crème Solférino.

☐ potato and leek   ☐ tomato and leek
☐ potato and tomato   ☐ potato and mushroom

25 What are the two French names for chicken soup?

1 Crème de   2 Crème

26 Describe the flavour of mulligatawny soup:

27 Which garnish is served with mulligatawny soup?

☐ croûtons   ☐ chicken
☐ rice   ☐ royale

28 Briefly explain the preparation of brown onion soup.

29 Describe how brown onion soup is served.

30 A flute is:

☐ diced fried bread   ☐ long thin loaf
☐ a roll   ☐ a cheese straw

31 What have kidney soup, thick mock turtle soup and thick oxtail soup in common?

32 Name the soup which is garnished with prunes, chicken and leek.

☐ cock-a-leekie   ☐ minestroni
☐ potage paysanne   ☐ mulligatawny

33★ Minestroni originates from

☐ Spain   ☐ France
☐ Portugal   ☐ Italy

34 What are the accompaniments to minestroni?

35 What does the term bisque indicate?

36★ Suggest four soups suitable for lunch.

1   2

3   4

37★ Suggest four suitable soups for dinner.

1   2

3   4

8
Eggs

pages 129–135

1* Describe how scrambled eggs should look when served.

2 When cooking scrambled eggs what points need particular attention?

3 Name five suitable garnishes for scrambled eggs.

1   2   3

4   5

4 How long does it take to cook egg in cocotte?

☐ 1–2 minutes   ☐ 3–4 minutes
☐ 2–3 minutes   ☐ 4–5 minutes

5 Suggest three suitable garnishes for egg in cocotte.

1   2   3

6 Match the appropriate cooking method of eggs to the approximate cooking time.

☐ hard-boiled eggs   1 3–5 minutes
☐ soft-boiled eggs   2 8–10 minutes
☐ boiled egg   3 5½ minutes

7 Suggest four ways of using hard-boiled eggs.

1   3

2   4

8 Explain how you would serve Scotch eggs:

1 Hot

2 Cold

9★ At which meal is a boiled egg served?

☐ breakfast   ☐ dinner
☐ lunch   ☐ supper

10 Describe a properly cooked poached egg:

11 Why is vinegar added to water when poaching eggs?

12 Match the following garnish with the appropriate dish

☐ poached egg florentine   1 sweetcorn
☐ poached egg Bombay   2 spinach
☐ poached egg à la reine   3 curry
☐ poached egg Washington   4 chicken

13 Why is it essential to use fresh eggs for poaching?

14 List five points which must be observed to produce a good omelet.

1   2   3

4   5

15 Name three flat omelets:

1   2   3

16 What is the garnish for each of the omelets named above?

1   2   3

17 How does the finished appearance of a jam omelet differ from a savoury one? (*Ans. p. 421*)

18★ What is the price of eggs?

19 In which would be served:

An omelet .... Egg in cocotte .... Oeuf sur le plat ....

9
Farinaceous Dishes

pages 144–145

1 What are farinaceous dishes?

2 At which meal is the farinaceous course usually part of the menu?

3* Why are farinaceous dishes so called?

4 Why is it necessary to cook spaghetti in plenty of boiling salted water?

5 Which of the following is usually served separately with farinaceous dishes?

    ☐ croûtons   ☐ cheese
    ☐ sippets   ☐ rice

6 What points need particular attention when cooking pasta?

7 Give the names of four farinaceous dishes.

    1   2

    3   4

8 From which country do farinaceous dishes originate?

    ☐ France   ☐ Spain
    ☐ Italy   ☐ Hungary

9 Which of the following is best served with farinaceous dishes?

    ☐ Cheddar   ☐ Gruyère
    ☐ Parmesan   ☐ Roquefort

10 What is the garnish used for spaghetti napolitaine?

11 List three items used to garnish spaghetti milanaise.

 1   2   3

12 What shape is the garnish milanaise?

 ☐ brunoise   ☐ paysanne
 ☐ jardinière   ☐ julienne

13 What is the main ingredient for bolognaise sauce?

 ☐ cheese   ☐ minced beef
 ☐ tomatoes   ☐ mushrooms

14 What is the French word for noodles?

15 Into what shape are noodles cut?

16 Puff paste is used to produce ravioli. true/false.

17 Explain the difference between canneloni and ravioli.

18 Name four dishes using pasta as a garnish.

 1   2

 3   4

19 Gnocchi means

 ☐ pasta   ☐ bun
 ☐ gnome   ☐ dumpling

20 Name three gnocchi and state the main ingredient of each.

 1

 2

 3

21★ Why is it necessary to simmer gnocchi gently?

22   What is the difference between riz pilaff and risotto?

23   List four points which need particular attention when cooking riz
     pilaff so as to achieve a good result.

     1   2

     3   4

24   Why is long-grained rice used for riz pilaff?

25   Name two rice dishes which are included in the farinaceous course of
     the menu.

     1   2

26   Which of the following is not a farinaceous dish?

     ☐ ravioli   ☐ spaghetti italienne
     ☐ canneloni   ☐ brindisi au beurre

27   Match the appropriate sauce with the correct dish:

     ☐ béchamel   1 spaghetti bolognaise
     ☐ tomato   2 macaroni cheese
     ☐ demi-glace   3 spaghetti napolitaine

28★ What is the cost per ½kg (1 lb) for

     1 vermicelli   2 macaroni
     3 spaghetti

29★ Cost four portions of macaroni au gratin.

30★ Put the numbers of the shape against the item

Vermicelli	Macaroni	Spaghetti
Canneloni	Ravioli	Pâté d'italie

31 Which item would you use for:

1 Grooving cucumber   3 Cutting ravioli
2 Peeling pears   4 Producing parisienne potatoes

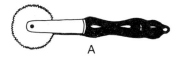

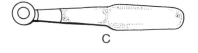

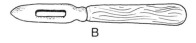

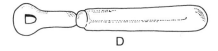

10
Fish

pages 155–158

1 Give three examples of white fish.

1   2   3

2 Which is the odd one and why?

☐ halibut   ☐ herring
☐ hake   ☐ haddock

3 Name three shellfish.

1   2   3

4 List five quality points for fish.

1   2   3

4   5

5 Which is suitable for boiling?

☐ sprats   ☐ salmon
☐ sole   ☐ herring

6 Explain how fish are boiled:

7 What is a court bouillon?

☐ royal stock   ☐ fish stock
☐ boiling kettle   ☐ liquid for cooking oily fish

8 What are the ingredients used in the making of a court bouillon?

9 Explain how fish are poached.

10 What term is applied to shallow fried fish?

☐ sauté ☐ darne
☐ goujons ☐ meunière

11 What is the reason for selecting a specific side to be cooked first when shallow-frying fillets of fish?

☐ appearance is better ☐ cooks more quickly
☐ cooks more evenly ☐ portion looks larger

12 Which side of a fillet is placed in the fat first when being shallow fried?

13 Describe three coatings for deep fried fish and explain the reason for coating fish before deep frying.

14 List seven French terms for the cuts of fish with the gender (le or la):

1   2

3   4

5   6

7

15 Name and describe each cut of fish from Question 14 in English.

English name   *Description*

1

2

3

4

5

6

7

16 How much fish is allowed per portion? (*Ans. p. 158*)

On the bone   Off the bone

17 Fish velouté is used for

☐ fish stock   ☐ fish sauces
☐ fish glaze   ☐ fish cocktail

18 What is the base for a sabayon?

☐ uncooked yolks   ☐ cooked whole eggs
☐ cooked whites   ☐ uncooked whole eggs

19 Why may a sabayon be used in a fish sauce?

20 How is a sabayon made?

21★ What must one be careful to do when making a sabayon?

22 In industry what sauce could be used in place of a sabayon?

23 How would fillets of plaice meunière be finished for serving?

24 What is garnish belle meunière?

☐ shrimp, tomato, herring roe   ☐ mushrooms, shrimps, herring
                                   roe
☐ mushrooms, tomato, shrimp   ☐ mushrooms, tomato, herring
                                   roe

25 Match the French name with the correct ingredient in English for
three variations of poisson meunière

☐ Grenobloise   1 cucumber
☐ Doria   2 shrimps and sliced mushrooms
☐ Bretonne   3 lemon segments and capers

26 Explain the preparation of herring for grilling.

27 How should grilled fish be finished and presented for service?

28 Mustard sauce would be served with:

☐ soused herrings   ☐ shallow fried herrings
☐ grilled herrings   ☐ deep fried herrings

29 How does the preparation of grilled fish St Germain differ from that of other fish?

30 A fish dish garnished with banana is called:

☐ Colère   ☐ Colbert
☐ Caprice   ☐ Cardinal

31 Name three raising agents that may be used in frying batters:

1

2

3

32 Compile a list of six points to ensure safety when deep frying fish. (*Ans. p 39*)

1   2

3   4

5   6

33 Describe how deep fried fish is served.

34 Which sauce may be served with crumbed deep fried fish?

☐ egg   ☐ parsley
☐ tartar   ☐ demi glace

35* Curled whiting is prepared in an unusual way. Explain this process.

36 What size are filets de sole en goujons and why are they so called?

1   2

37   Explain the preparation and presentation of sole colbert.

38   The marinade for fried fish à l'Orly consists of:

39   The temperature of the fat in which whitebait are cooked is:
☐ 105°C   ☐ 175°C
☐ 125°C   ☐ 195°C

40   Whitebait are served with their heads on: true/false.

41   What is the English term for young turbot?

42   The French for young turbot is:
☐ turbotin   ☐ thon
☐ truite   ☐ turbot

43★ Describe the difference between brill and turbot.

44   When turbot is cut on the bone what is it called?
☐ darne   ☐ tronçon
☐ suprême   ☐ goujon

45   Would you write on the menu 'filet de turbot?' Yes/no.

46★ Explain the reasons for your answer to question 45.

47   What is the name given to a cut of salmon on the bone?
☐ tronçon   ☐ filet
☐ suprême   ☐ darne

48   Which of the following accompanies hot cooked salmon?
☐ sliced cucumber   ☐ grated carrot
☐ grated cheese   ☐ sliced truffle

49   Name 3 flat fish which may be used for boiling:
1   2   3

50★ When cooking whole fish in a liquid, why should the liquid be only allowed to simmer gently?

51★ When poaching fish why is only the minimum of liquid used?

52 What garnish is served with a fish dish named Véronique?

☐ bananas   ☐ grapes
☐ oranges   ☐ apples

53 a) What is the garnish Bercy?
b) What is added to it to become bonne femme?
c) What is added to bonne femme to become Bréval (d'Antin)?

a)   b)   c)

54 Which of the following are glazed:

☐ filets de sole vin blanc   ☐ filets de sole Marguery
☐ filets de sole Bercy   ☐ filets de sole Bréval

55 Which of the following are gratinated?

☐ filets de sole Mornay   ☐ filets de sole Walewska
☐ filets de sole florentine   ☐ filets de sole d'Antin

56 What is kedgeree?

57 Which fish is sometimes served with black butter and capers?

☐ halibut   ☐ skate
☐ plaice   ☐ salmon

58 What method of cookery is employed for cooking the dish in question 57?

59 Suggest three ways of using cooked fish.

1

2

3

60 Mayonnaise de saumon and salade de saumon are served differently; explain how they are served.

61 If half a lobster is served for a portion, a 1 kg (2 lb) lobster would be ordered: true/false.

62 Explain the significance of using the words *fillet* and *fillets* on the menu.

63 How should mussels be prepared prior to cooking?

☐ salted and drained   ☐ blanched and drained
☐ washed and filleted   ☐ scraped and washed

64 Why should the raw mussel shells be tightly closed?

65 How may scallop shells be opened?

☐ on top of the stove   ☐ under the salamander
☐ in boiling water   ☐ in a steamer

66 What sort of potato is piped round the edge of a scallop shell for scallop with cheese sauce? (*Ans. p. 176*)

☐ mashed   ☐ purée
☐ duchess   ☐ creamed

67★ What is the price of:

herrings   plaice (whole)

turbot   plaice (filleted)

68★ What is the price of:

lobster   scallops

69 Correct the names of these cuts of fish:

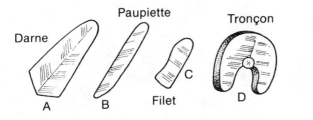

Darne   Paupiette   Tronçon   Filet   Suprême
A   B   C   D   E

11
Lamb and Mutton

pages 186–189

1 Approximately how much lamb on the bone and how much off the bone is calculated per head when ordering?

On the bone   Off the bone

2 What is the difference between lamb and mutton?

3 Name the joints and their uses.

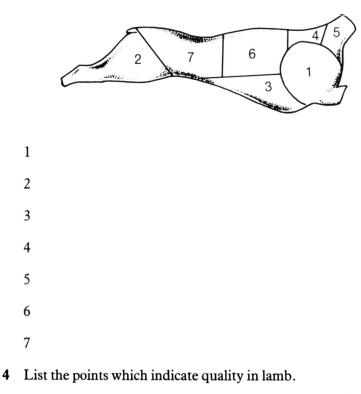

    1

    2

    3

    4

    5

    6

    7

4 List the points which indicate quality in lamb.

5   List the small cuts of lamb.

6   State from which joints the small cuts are obtained.

7   The tail end of the saddle is called the ....

8   A saddle divided into two lengthwise produces two ....

9   When skinning a saddle it is best to skin from tail to head and back to breast: true/false.

10 Why is the surface of the saddle of lamb scored?
    ☐ for ease of carving   ☐ to shorten cooking time
    ☐ to allow fat to flow out   ☐ to assist basting

11 How is a noisette of lamb prepared?

12 List the offal obtained from a carcass of lamb.

13 Which joints of lamb may be cooked by roasting?

14 Name two kinds of lamb chops
    1   2

15 Which lamb joints are suitable for stuffing?
    ☐ leg   ☐ best end
    ☐ shoulder   ☐ loin

16 Which sauce is suitable for serving with roast lamb?

17 Which sauce is served with roast mutton?
    ☐ onion   ☐ horseradish
    ☐ cranberry   ☐ apple

18 Which jelly is traditionally served with roast mutton?
    ☐ cranberry   ☐ quince
    ☐ orange   ☐ redcurrant

19 The best end is cut into chops: true/false. (*Ans. p. 191*)

20 List the usual ingredients in a mixed grill.

21 Describe the preparation of lamb cutlets for cutlets reform.

22 What sauce is traditionally served with boiled leg of mutton?
☐ parsley   ☐ egg
☐ caper   ☐ mushroom

23 From what liquor is this sauce made?

24 What is a kebab, how is it cooked, and with what is it usually served?
1   2   3

25 What do you understand by toad in the hole? (*Ans. p. 260*)

26 Suggest three ways of serving lamb chops.
1   2   3

27 Name and describe four suitable garnishes for serving with noisette of lamb.
1   2

3   4

28★ What is the filet mignon?
☐ the top of the leg
☐ the equivalent joint to the nut of veal
☐ the equivalent joint to the fillet of beef
☐ boned out shoulder

29 Name four different varieties of lamb stew.
1   2

3   4

30 What do the words *navarin* and *ragoût* indicate?

31 What does 'turned' mean when applied to vegetables?
☐ shaped like a barrel   ☐ canned vegetables
☐ shaken in the pan   ☐ finished in butter

32 How are turned vegetables produced glacé? (*Ans. p 224*)

33 Long grain rice is used for plain boiled rice: true/false.

34 What points distinguish high standards for plain boiled rice?

35 How is a high standard of plain boiled rice achieved?

36 List a selection of items which may accompany curried lamb.

37 Bombay Duck is roasted: true/false.

38 Describe popadums and explain how they are cooked and served.

1

2

3

39* What is the cost of popadums?

40 What is desiccated coconut?

41* What is the cost of desiccated coconut?

42 What is moussaka?

43 From what country does moussaka originate?
☐ Italy   ☐ Turkey
☐ Russia   ☐ Greece

44 Suggest three dishes using cooked lamb:

1   2   3

45 Name four items of lamb offal and suggest a suitable dish for each.

1   2

3   4

46★ Why must sautéd kidneys be fried quickly?

☐ to prevent loss of juices   ☐ to increase flavour
☐ to remove strong flavour   ☐ to shrink them

47 The garnish turbigo consists of button mushrooms and chipolatas: true/false.

48 Suggest two ways of serving lambs' sweetbreads.

1   2

49 Delete the incorrect names

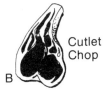

A   Chop / Cutlet

B   Cutlet / Chop

50 From which joint are A cutlets, B chops obtained?

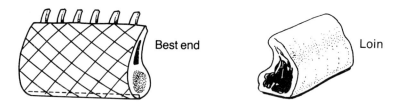

Best end   Loin

12
Beef

pages 210–213

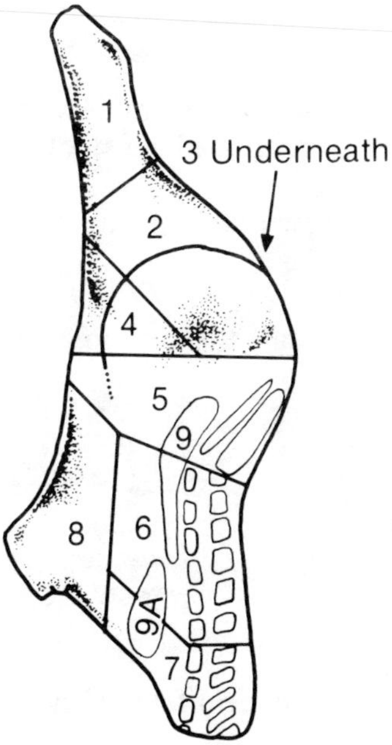

1 Name the joints and their uses.

1

2

3

4

5

6

7

8

9

3 Underneath

9A

2 Name the joints and their uses.

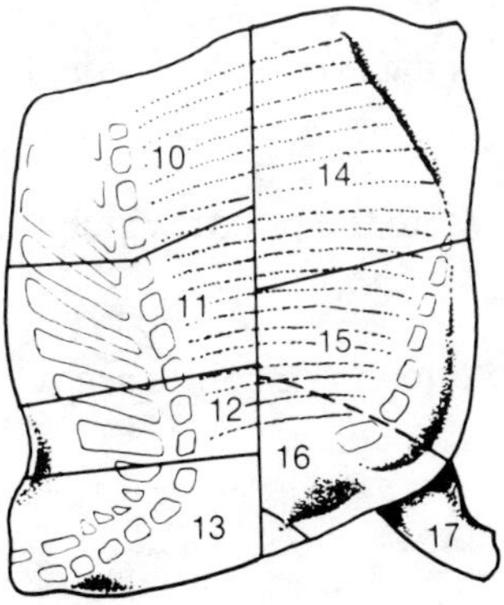

10

11

12

13

14

15

16

17

3 List the points of quality in beef.

4 Suggest a suitable order for dissecting a hindquarter.

5 What is brine? (*Ans. p. 46*)

6 What is brine used for?
- ☐ salting silverside of beef
- ☐ straining beef stock
- ☐ seasoning beef stews
- ☐ shrinking string on beef

7 Name the small cuts of beef obtained from sirloin.

8 Indicate the cuts on a fillet of beef and name them.

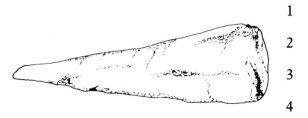

1

2

3

4

9 Name the offal obtained from a carcass of beef.

10 Which is the most suitable joint for roasting?
- ☐ silverside
- ☐ chuck steak
- ☐ thick flank
- ☐ sirloin

11 What are the traditional accompaniments for roast beef?

12 State the points which indicate when a joint of beef is cooked.

13 Which vegetables are served with French style boiled beef?

14 Which two items usually accompany boiled beef French style?

☐ capers and coarse salt

☐ pickled gherkins and coarse salt

☐ pickled red cabbage and French mustard

☐ pickled gherkins and French mustard

15 Name six steaks and state from which joint they are obtained.

1   2

3   4

5   6

16 Name four degrees of grilling steaks in both English and French.

1   2

3   4

17 What is the usual garnish served with grilled steak?

18* Roast gravy is served with grilled meat: true/false.

19 Garnish Henry IV comprises:

☐ watercress and pommes pont neuf

☐ watercress and pommes frites

☐ watercress and pommes pailles

☐ watercress and pommes allumettes

20 A point steak is cut from the:

☐ sirloin

☐ wing rib

☐ fillet

☐ rump

21 Suggest four suitable garnishes for sautéd tournedos.

1   2

3   4

22* Why is a brown beef stew served in an entrée dish?

23 Which of the following would you use in a beef stew with red wine?

☐ hock ☐ claret
☐ chablis ☐ marsala

24 Which of the following cuts would you use for beef Stroganoff?

☐ fillet ☐ thick flank
☐ topside ☐ sirloin

25 Why have you chosen this cut for beef Stroganoff?

26 Which of the following is an ingredient for carbonnade of beef?

☐ vichy water ☐ beer
☐ wine ☐ cider

27 Which of the following is used in goulash?

☐ paprika ☐ cayenne
☐ pimento ☐ cinnamon

28 Goulash is garnished with gnocchi: true/false.

29 Before serving paupiettes the .... must be removed.

30 What is the English for paupiettes de boeuf?

31 Name two cuts of beef suitable for braising.

1   2

32 Braised beef is cut with the grain or across the grain?

33★ Why have you answered question 32 in this way?

34 How do you know if the joint of braised beef is cooked?

35 Suggest three suitable garnishes for braised beef.

1   2   3

36 Which paste is used for making dumplings?

☐ suet   ☐ choux
☐ short   ☐ noodle

37 How may minced beef be presented in an attractive manner?

38 With which kind of meat would you make Vienna steaks?

☐ lean minced beef   ☐ cooked meat
☐ lean minced lamb   ☐ venison

39 Croquettes, cutlets, and Vienna steaks; which is the correct shape for each?

40 Which wine is usually added to the sauce served with braised ox tongue?

☐ madeira   ☐ sherry
☐ marsala   ☐ port

41 An ox tongue will cook in approximately:

☐ 1–2 hours   ☐ 3–4 hours
☐ 2–3 hours   ☐ 4–5 hours

42 Braised ox liver requires .... hours simmering to become tender.

43 400g (1 lb) of tripe to 200g (½lb) onions are needed to produce four portions: true/false.

44 Which pulse is used to garnish oxtail?

☐ lentils   ☐ haricot beans
☐ butter beans   ☐ yellow split peas

45 What is the approximate cooking time for oxtail?

46★ What is the price of fillet of beef?

47★ What is the cost of oxtail?

48★ Is ox liver more expensive than lamb's liver?

49★ How much does minced beef cost?

50 Which fish could be used in steak and kidney pudding?

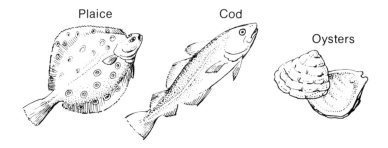

Plaice   Cod   Oysters

51 Which item would be used for passing flour?

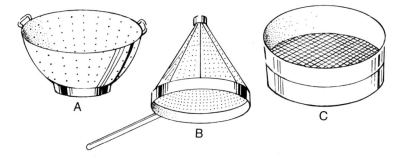

A   B   C

52 Name a suitable paste and meat filling for each item:

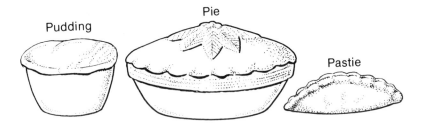

Pudding   Pie   Pastie

13
Veal

pages 237–240

1 Place the joints in their correct positions by inserting numbers in the diagram.

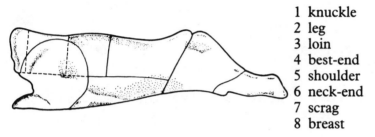

1 knuckle
2 leg
3 loin
4 best-end
5 shoulder
6 neck-end
7 scrag
8 breast

2 The average weight of a Dutch milk fed leg of veal is:

☐ 9kg (18lbs)   ☐ 15kg (3)lbs)
☐ 12kg (24lbs)   ☐ 18kg (36lbs)

3 The proportion of bone in a leg of veal is approximately:

☐ 7%   ☐ 21%
☐ 14%   ☐ 28%

4 The proportion of meat in a leg of veal suitable for escalopes is:

☐ 20%   ☐ 36%
☐ 30%   ☐ 46%

5 Which of the following is used for osso buco?

☐ leg   ☐ breast
☐ loin   ☐ knuckle

6 Calves' liver is one of the most suitable livers for frying: true/false.

7 The corresponding veal joint to topside of beef is ....

8 The corresponding veal joint to silverside of beef is ....

9 The corresponding veal joint to thick flank of beef is ....

10 When dissecting a leg of veal, the knuckle is removed first: true/false.

11★ The anticipated yield of 100g (4 oz) escalopes from a 18kg (36lb) leg of veal would be:

☐ 65 ☐ 45
☐ 55 ☐ 35

12 What colour is the flesh of good quality veal?

13 Flesh of good quality veal should be firm in structure, not soft or flabby: true/false.

14 When preparing osso buco, shin of veal should be cut:

☐ 2–3cm (1–1½in) ☐ 3–4cm (1½–2in)
☐ 1–1½cm (½–¾in) ☐ 4–6cm (2–3in)

15★ Why should veal sweetbreads be well washed, blanched, and trimmed before being used?

16 A brown veal stew is known as:

☐ ragoût ☐ blanquette
☐ navarin ☐ fricassée

17 For a blanquette of veal the meat is cooked in stock: true/false.

18 For a fricassée of veal, the meat is cooked in sauce: true/false.

19 Any white stew of veal may be finished with a liaison of:

20 A fricassée of veal may be finished by adding a few drops of lemon juice: true/false.

21 Garnish à l'ancienne consists of:

☐ button onions and button   ☐ button onions and tomatoes
    mushrooms   ☐ button onions and
☐ button onions and lardons   courgettes

22 Which of the following pastes would you use to cover a hot veal and ham pie?

☐ short ☐ hot water
☐ rough puff or puff ☐ choux

23 When preparing a stuffing for veal olives, the finely chopped meat trimmings can be added: true/false.

24 The best veal escalopes are cut from the .... or .... of veal?

25* Which of the following is most suitable for frying veal escalopes?

☐ lard ☐ olive oil
☐ margarine ☐ oil and butter

26 Which of the following veal escalopes would be garnished with a fried egg and anchovy fillets?

☐ viennoise ☐ napolitaine
☐ à la crème ☐ Holstein

27 Which ingredients are sandwiched in between two slices of veal in veal escalopes cordon bleu?

☐ bacon and mushroom ☐ tongue and ham
☐ bacon and cheese ☐ ham and cheese

28 Veal escalopes with cream are pané (flour, egg and crumbed): true/false.

29 Veal escalopes with madeira are lightly floured before cooking: true/false.

30 What additions are usually made when roasting a leg of veal in order to increase flavour?

31 Roast gravy served with veal is traditionally:

☐ thin ☐ thickened

32 Traditional garnish with roast leg of veal is:

☐ parsley and thyme stuffing and thinly sliced ham
☐ sage and onion stuffing and thinly sliced ham
☐ parsley and chive stuffing and chipolata sausage
☐ parsley and thyme stuffing and chipolata sausage

33 Veal stuffing usually contains chopped suet: true/false.

34 Which of the following is more traditionally used in the cooking of osso buco?

☐ marsala   ☐ madeira
☐ red wine   ☐ dry white wine

35 Which of the following is usually served with calf's liver and bacon?

☐ tomato sauce   ☐ devilled sauce
☐ mustard sauce   ☐ jus lié

36 What are sweetbreads?

☐ glands   ☐ nerves
☐ muscles   ☐ joints

37 Which sweetbread is of superior quality?

☐ throat   ☐ stomach

38 Veal sweetbreads may be braised white or brown: true/false.

39★ Veal sweetbreads are only suitable for serving braised white: true/false.

40 Which would you consider to be a suitable garnish for fried breadcrumbed veal escalopes?

☐ stuffed tomatoes   ☐ aubergine provençale
☐ grilled bacon   ☐ asparagus tips

41 Which is the most suitable dish for serving escalope of veal viennoise?

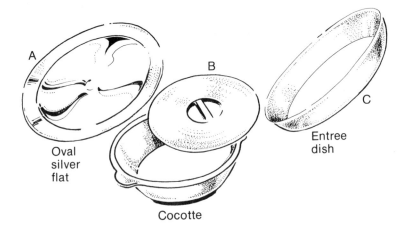

Oval
silver
flat

Cocotte

Entree
dish

14
Pork

pages 254–257

1 Name the joints in a side of pork:

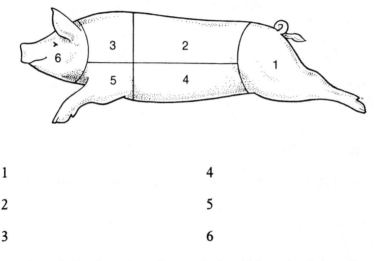

1   4

2   5

3   6

2 The lean flesh of good quality pork should be pale pink, soft and of a fine texture: true/false.

3 In order to be able to carve a leg of pork efficiently, it is not necessary to remove the aitch bone before the leg is cooked: true/false.

4 When scoring the rind of pork, how far apart should the incisions be?
   ☐ 2mm (⅛ in)   ☐ 2cm (1in)
   ☐ 1cm (½in)   ☐ 3cm (1½in)

5 Which of the following herbs is most suitable for seasoning a boned, rolled belly of pork for roasting?
   ☐ thyme   ☐ tarragon
   ☐ parsley   ☐ sage

6 In an oven at 230–250°C a leg of pork should be roasted for approximately:

☐ 10 minutes to the ½kg (1 lb) and 10 minutes over
☐ 15 minutes to the ½kg (1 lb) and 15 minutes over
☐ 20 minutes to the ½kg (1 lb) and 20 minutes over
☐ 25 minutes to the ½kg (1 lb) and 25 minutes over

7 Roast pork must always be well cooked: true/false.

8 The traditional accompaniments for roast pork are:

☐ roast gravy, orange sauce, sage and onion stuffing
☐ roast gravy, apple sauce, parsley and thyme stuffing
☐ roast gravy, prune sauce, sage and parsley stuffing
☐ roast gravy, apple sauce, sage and onion stuffing

9★ Ideally, sage and onion stuffing should be prepared using dripping from the pork joint: true/false.

10 Would you consider that a dish of pease pudding is suitable for serving with boiled pork? Yes/no.

11 Which of the following sauces would you consider most suitable for serving with a grilled pork chop?

☐ tomato   ☐ parsley
☐ apple   ☐ tartare

12 Which of the following would be cooked in with a dish of pork chops à la flamande?

☐ red cabbage   ☐ apples
☐ peas   ☐ tomatoes

13 Which of the following pork joints is most suitable for barbecues?

☐ spare ribs   ☐ shoulder
☐ loin   ☐ leg

14★ Brawn is made from the pig's:

☐ head   ☐ heart
☐ liver   ☐ trimmings

15★ Brawn is an economical cold meat preparation: true/false.

16 Traditional seasoning for raised pork pies is:

☐ rosemary, nutmeg, clove   ☐ sage, allspice
☐ parsley, cinnamon, chive   ☐ onion, parsley, tarragon

17 Raised pork pies may be served hot or cold: true/false.

18 Traditional seasoning for veal and ham pie is:

☐ lemon, chive, clove   ☐ lemon, parsley, sage
☐ lemon, cinnamon, parsley   ☐ lemon, parsley, thyme

19 Forcemeat is a term given to:

☐ numerous mixtures of meats
☐ sausage meat before putting into skins
☐ stuffing for roast pork joints
☐ a mince made from a meat substitute

20★ What is the price of a leg of pork per ½kg (1 lb)?

21★ What is the price of shoulder of pork per ½kg (1 lb)?

22★ What is the price of loin of pork per ½kg (1 lb)?

23★ What is the price of spare rib of pork per ½kg (1 lb)?

24★ Which would be used to produce brawn?

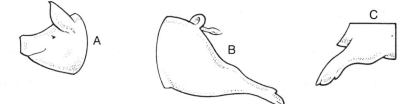

15
Bacon

pages 263–265

1 Fill in the names of the joints on the side of bacon.

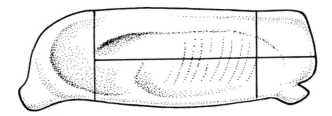

2★ What is the price of prime gammon per ½kg (1lb)?

3★ What is the price of back rashers per ½kg (1 lb)?

4★ What is the price of streaky bacon per ½kg (1 lb)?

5 The approximate weight of a gammon is:

☐ 2½kg (5 lb) ☐ 7½kg (15lb)
☐ 5kg (10lb) ☐ 10kg (20lb)

6 In assessing quality, the lean of bacon should be a deep pink colour and firm: true/false.

7 In assessing quality, the fat should be white, smooth and not excessive in proportion to the lean: true/false.

8 What is the most popular cut of bacon for frying?

☐ collar ☐ hock ☐ streaky

9 Gammon rashers for grilling should be cut as thinly as possible: true/false.

10 When preparing hock of bacon for boiling, in order to facilitate carving, it is best to leave all bones in: true/false.

11 Before boiling a bacon joint should:

☐ not be soaked   ☐ be soaked in water for 12 hours

☐ be soaked in stock   ☐ be soaked in water for 24 hours

12 When boiling bacon allow per ½kg (1 lb):

☐ 10 minutes + 10 minutes over   ☐ 20 minutes + 20 minutes over

☐ 15 minutes + 15 minutes over   ☐ 25 minutes + 25 minutes over

13 Boiled bacon should be removed from the cooking liquor as soon as it is cooked: true/false.

14 What is the traditional sauce for serving with hot boiled bacon?

☐ tomato   ☐ chestnut
☐ apple   ☐ parsley

15 Which of the following accompaniments is most traditional for serving with hot boiled bacon?

☐ macaroni cheese   ☐ buttered swede
☐ mashed turnips   ☐ pease pudding

16 Grilled gammon rashers should only be served for breakfast: true/false.

17 In order to carve a ham efficiently and help to keep the slices intact, it is better to leave the aitch bone in: true/false.

18 Which of the following hams is so prepared that it can be sliced thinly and eaten raw?

☐ Polish   ☐ Wiltshire
☐ Danish   ☐ Parma

19 When serving smoked ham in England, would it be usual to serve it for:

☐ breakfast   ☐ hors-d'oeuvre
☐ tea   ☐ for supper with fried eggs

page 266

20 A ham is cut from a side of pork: true/false.

21 A gammon is cut from a side of pork: true/false.

22 A gammon and ham – which is which?

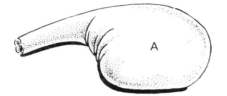

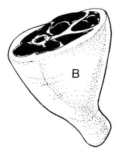

16
Poultry and Game

pages 268–274

1   The largest chicken suitable for roasting is a capon: true/false.

2   The approximate weight of a baby chicken (poussin) is:
   ☐ 150g (¼lb)   ☐ ¾kg (1½lb)
   ☐ 1 kg (2lb)   ☐ 1½kg (3lb)

3   List four signs of quality in chicken.

   1   2

   3   4

4★ What is the price of prime roasting chicken per ½kg (1 lb)?

5★ What is the price of old boiling fowl per ½kg (1 lb)?

6   When preparing a chicken for roasting the wishbone may be removed in order to facilitate carving: true/false.

7   The traditional method of cutting a chicken into pieces for sauté yields 2 drumsticks, 2 thighs, 2 wings, 2 breasts and the carcass: true/false.

8   The most suitable weight of chicken for cutting suprême is:
   ☐ ¾–1 kg (1½–2lb)   ☐ 1¼–1½kg (2½–3lb)
   ☐ 2–3kg (4–6lb)

9   When preparing suprêmes of chicken is the skin left:
   ☐ on   ☐ off

10★ Why is it more efficient to remove the wishbone from a chicken before removing the suprêmes?

11 A ballottine is:

☐ a boned stuffed leg of chicken   ☐ a brown stew of chicken legs
☐ a ball shaped chicken cutlet   ☐ a kitchen knife for cutting ball
                                        shaped pieces

12 List four signs of quality in ducks.

1   2

3   4

13★ What is the price of prime duck per ½kg (1 lb)?

14 What is the approximate weight of a goose?

☐ 2 kg (4 lb)   ☐ 3 kg (6 lb)
☐ 4 kg (8 lb)   ☐ 6 kg (12 lb)

15 Turkeys are available in weights from 3½–20 kg (7–40 lb): true/false.

16 Which is the traditional stuffing for turkey?

☐ breadcrumbs and parsley   ☐ sausage meat and chestnuts
☐ forcemeat and sage   ☐ breadcrumbs and chestnuts

17 Which are the traditional accompaniments for roast turkey?

☐ roast gravy, bread sauce, cranberry sauce, chipolatas, bacon
☐ roast gravy, white sauce, apple sauce, sausage, ham
☐ roast gravy, parsley sauce, tomato sauce, chipolatas, bacon
☐ roast gravy, bread sauce, cranberry sauce, ham, bacon

18 Which of the following weights of raw dressed bird are required to
yield four good portions of raw chicken?
☐ ¾–1 kg (1½–2lb)   ☐ ½–¾ kg (1–1½lb)
☐ 1¼–1½ kg (3lb)   ☐ 2–2½ kg (4–5lb)

19 When a roast chicken is cooked there should be slight signs of blood
in the juice issuing from it: true/false.

20 When preparing a stuffing for roast chicken the chopped raw chicken
liver may be added: true/false.

21 What ingredients would you use to make the devil mixture for grilled devilled chicken?

1   2

3   4

22 Is a chicken spatchcock:

☐ boiled   ☐ roast
☐ fried   ☐ grilled

23 When preparing a jus-lié or demi-glace for use with a chicken sauté, the chicken giblets should not be used as they may taint the sauce: true/false.

24 Which of the following are typical ingredients of chicken sauté chasseur?

☐ mushrooms, bacon, tomatoes ☐ mushrooms, tomatoes,
                                 tarragon
☐ tomatoes, courgettes, parsley ☐ tomatoes, rice, tarragon

25 When cooking pieces of chicken for a sauté, indicate with numbers 1–4 in which order you would put them into the pan.

☐ thighs   ☐ wings
☐ drumsticks   ☐ breasts
   ⋆ Why?

26 When cooking suprême de volaille à la crème, the suprêmes should be lightly floured and cooked in butter with the minimum amount of colour: true/false.

27 When preparing suprême de volaille aux pointes d'asperges it is usual to pané the suprêmes: true/false.

28 Which of the following rice dishes is usually served with boiled chicken and suprême sauce?

☐ risotto with short grain rice ☐ pilaf with short grain rice
☐ risotto with long grain rice   ☐ pilaf with long grain rice

29 Which of the following are typical of chicken à la king?

☐ red pimento, mushrooms, marsala   ☐ red pimento, mushrooms, sherry

☐ green pimento, mushrooms, red wine   ☐ green pimento, mushrooms, white wine

30★ When preparing chicken vol-au-vent, the chicken mixture should be put into the puff pastry cases well in advance of service in order to let the flavour soak into the pastry: true/false.

31 Chicken cutlets must always be deep fried: true/false.

32 When preparing a fricassée of chicken, the pieces of chicken should be cooked in with the sauce: true/false.

33 Which of the following are the more usual ingredients in a chicken pie?

☐ mushroom, bacon, hard-boiled egg, parsley
☐ onions, carrots, leeks, celery
☐ mushrooms, carrots, hard-boiled egg, sage
☐ onions, rosemary, tomatoes, courgettes.

34 A chicken salad would normally be accompanied by a mayonnaise sauce: true/false.

35 When preparing a curry of chicken, the curry powder should be diluted in water and added to the dish for the last few minutes of cooking only: true/false.

36 Which of the following is the traditional accompaniment to a curry of chicken?

☐ plain boiled rice, raw sliced mushrooms, bacon
☐ pilaf rice, sliced tomatoes, grated cheese
☐ pilaf rice, boiled ham, chutney
☐ plain boiled rice, grilled poppadums and bombay duck

37 What are the traditional accompaniments for English roast duck?

☐ sage and onion stuffing and cranberry sauce
☐ thyme and parsley stuffing and cranberry sauce
☐ sage and onion stuffing and apple sauce
☐ thyme and parsley stuffing and apple sauce

38 When preparing orange salad to serve with roast duck would you cut the oranges into:

☐ segments free from skin and   ☐ slices free from skin and pips
    pips   ☐ quarters with skin and rind on
☐ slices with skins and rind on

39 It is not necessary to stone cherries for duckling with cherries: true/false.

40 Which of the following is cooked in with braised duck and peas?

☐ lardons, button onions, peas   ☐ lardons, chipolatas, peas
☐ ham, chipolatas, peas   ☐ carrots, turnips, peas

41 What is venison?

42 What type of meat is venison?

☐ dry and tough   ☐ moist and tough
☐ dry and tender   ☐ moist and tender

43 Describe two procedures which help to overcome the dryness and toughness in venison.

1

2

44 A carcass of venison should be hung for approximately:

☐ 1–2 days   ☐ 8–9 days
☐ 5–6 days   ☐ 12–21 days

45 List six vegetables and herbs used in a marinade.

1   2   3

4   5   6

46 Are good class joints of venison obtained from the fore or hindquarter?

47 Name the most suitable accompaniment for a hot roast haunch of venison.

☐ roast gravy   ☐ piquante sauce
☐ jus lié   ☐ Cumberland sauce

48 Which would be the most traditional sauce to accompany a cold roast of venison?

☐ vinaigrette   ☐ tomato ketchup
☐ mayonnaise   ☐ Cumberland

49★ Compare the prices of venison and beef.

50 To test for age, the ear of a young hare should tear easily between the fingers: true/false.

51★ What is the price of a young hare?

52 After killing, and before cleaning, a hare should be hung for approximately:

☐ 1–2 days   ☐ 6–7 days
☐ 3–4 days   ☐ 10–11 days

53 A brown stew of hare is known as:

☐ ragoût   ☐ fricassée
☐ sauté   ☐ civet

54 What is the traditional English term for a brown stew of hare?

55 Why is the blood saved when preparing a brown stew of hare?

56 The dish in question 53 should be garnished with:

☐ button onions, button   ☐ button onions, button
    mushrooms, lardons   mushrooms, rice
☐ button onions, tomatoes, peas ☐ button mushrooms, lardons,
                                   peas

57 Heart-shaped croûtons spread with redcurrant jelly should also garnish the dish: true/false.

58 Give the English translation for the following

faisan   *bécasse*

perdreau   *bécassine*

canard sauvage

59 How can you improve the flavour of most game birds before preparing and cooking them?

60 What happens to the flesh of game birds during the hanging process?

61 Game birds should be plucked before being hung: true/false.

62 What type of game bird should *not* be hung for too long?

63 What do we mean when we say a game bird is 'high'?

64 Name five ingredients used in making a game farce.

1   2   3

4   5

65* Why should you tie a piece of fat bacon over the breast of a game bird before roasting?

66 What are the traditional accompaniments to a roast game bird?

67 A partridge should be hung for:

☐ 1–2 days   ☐ 7–9 days
☐ 3–5 days   ☐ 10–12 days

68 Which game bird has the cleaned entrails left in during cooking in order to enhance the flavour?

☐ pheasant   ☐ grouse
☐ partridge   ☐ woodcock

69 Is a snipe larger or smaller than a woodcock?

70 Why is it particularly important that water game birds be eaten only in season?

71 What is a teal?

72 The grouse season is:
- ☐ August 1st – November 30th
- ☐ August 12th – December 10th
- ☐ August 30th – December 31st
- ☐ August 12th – January 31st

73 The approximate weight of a grouse is:
- ☐ 150g (6 oz)
- ☐ 300g (12 oz)
- ☐ 400g (1 lb)
- ☐ 600g (1½ lb)

74 Hot roast grouse is normally cooked slightly underdone? True/false

75 What is a salmis of game?

76★ What were the prices of the following game when last in season?

grouse   pheasant   partridge

77 Place the following in order of size from the smallest to the largest.

pheasant   snipe   partridge

78 Name the dishes   Give the *French* names for:
A   A
B   C
C

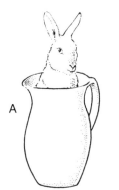

Scrambled egg

A   B   C   1000 leaves

79 For which dishes would bread cut in these shapes be used?

A C
B D

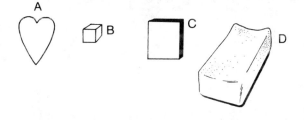

80 For which purpose in the larder would these be used?

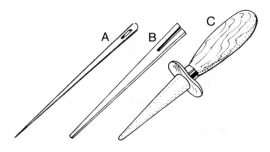

17
Vegetarian Dishes

pages 304–324

1   Very briefly explain the difference between a vegan and a vegetarian.

2   From what is soy sauce derived?

3   What is tofu?

4   Crudités are:

☐ crude oils
☐ raw vegetables
☐ oriental spices
☐ underdressed vegans

5   Match the following:

☐ Ratatouille   1 a source of oil
☐ Lentils   2 a vegetable dish
☐ Allspice   3 a pulse
☐ Sesame seed   4 a seasoning
☐ Smetana   5 a colouring
☐ Saffron   6 a dairy product

6   What is tvp?

7   Name six nuts

1   2   3

4   5   6

8   Outline the method for cooking dried beans, such as red kidney beans.

18
Vegetables

pages 325–330

1   Vegetables which grow above the ground should be started in boiling salted water: true/false.

2   As a general rule the cooking of all root vegetables with the exception of new potatoes is started in cold salted water: true/false.

3   Suggest a suitable sauce for serving with:

hot globe artichoke   cold globe artichoke

4   To cook a globe artichoke allow approximately:

☐ 5–10 minutes   ☐ 20–30 minutes
☐ 10–15 minutes   ☐ 40–45 minutes

5   Name the liquid in which artichokes bottoms are cooked.

6   Two types of artichoke are used in cookery. One is globe, name the other.

7★ What is the current price of a globe artichoke?

8★ What is the current price of a tin of artichoke bottoms?

9   How many pieces of asparagus are usually allowed per portion?

☐ 2–3   ☐ 6–8
☐ 4–5   ☐ 10–12

10   It is not necessary to wash asparagus before cooking: true/false.

11   Asparagus will cook in approximately:

☐ 5 minutes   ☐ 15 minutes
☐ 10 minutes   ☐ 20 minutes

12   Suggest two sauces for serving with hot asparagus.

    1   2

13   Asparagus is only served hot: true/false.

14★ What is the approximate price of fresh asparagus per ½kg (1 lb)?

15★ What is an approximate price of frozen asparagus per ½kg (1 lb)?

16   Young thin asparagus are known as ....

17   The French name for egg-plant is ....

18★ What is the price of aubergines?

19★ Could duxelle be used to stuff egg-plant?

    ☐ yes   ☐ no

20   What is ratatouille?

21   Broccoli may be cooked and served as for any cauliflower recipe: true/false.

22★ What is the price of fresh broccoli?

23★ What is the price of frozen broccoli?

24   When cooking buttered carrots, how would you glaze them?

25   Vichy carrots should be cooked in the same way as buttered carrots: true/false.

26★ What is the price of carrots?

27   What basic sauce would you use for carrots in cream sauce?

    ☐ velouté   ☐ hollandaise
    ☐ suprême   ☐ béchamel

28 To cook braised celery allow approximately:

☐ 1–1½ hours   ☐ 4–5 hours
☐ 2–3 hours   ☐ 6 hours

29★ What is the price of twelve heads of fresh celery?

30★ What is the price of twelve large tins of celery hearts?

31 The cooking liquor from braised celery is added to an equal amount of............... or .... in order to make the coating sauce.

32 ½kg (1 lb) cabbage will yield:

☐ 1–2 portions   ☐ 5–6 portions
☐ 3–4 portions   ☐ 7–8 portions

33★ What is the price of cabbage?

34 When cooking cabbage, state two factors which affect the vitamin content.

1   2

35 Suggest a suitable filling for braised stuffed cabbage.

36 Sauerkraut is:
☐ braised cabbage   ☐ German spring cabbage
☐ boiled white cabbage ☐ pickled white cabbage

37 Suggest four different ways of serving cauliflower.

1   2

3   4

38★ What is the price of a six-portion cauliflower?

39 Cauliflower polonaise is finished with:

☐ browned breadcrumbs, sieved ☐ breadcrumbs and cheese
    hard-boiled eggs and   ☐ butter, breadcrumbs and
    chopped parsley   parsley
☐ cheese sauce

40 Suggest two suitable sauces for serving with seakale.

1   2

41★ What is the price of seakale?

42 All variations for cooking and serving cauliflower may be used with marrow: true/false.

43★ What is the price of 20kg (40lb) marrow?

44 Translate the following:

courge

courgette

courge farcie

45 To prepare marrow Provençale you would add:

☐ chopped onion, garlic, tomatoes and parsley
☐ chopped onion, garlic, pimento and parsley
☐ chopped onion, mushrooms, parsley and garlic
☐ chopped onion, garlic, mushrooms and pimento

46 1kg (2lb) spinach will yield:

☐ 1 portion   ☐ 3 portions
☐ 2 portions   ☐ 4 portions

47 Spinach is a vegetable that needs a minimum washing: true/false.

48 The time required to cook spinach is approximately:

☐ 2 minutes   ☐ 10 minutes
☐ 5 minutes   ☐ 15 minutes

49★ What is the current market price of fresh spinach?

50★ What is the current market price of frozen spinach?

51 Before cooking haricot beans they may be soaked overnight in cold water: true/false.

52 Approximately how much of the following would you add when cooking 1kg (2lb) haricot beans?

carrot   onion   bacon trimmings

53 Translate the following:

haricot verts   épinards

fèves   endive

54 To cook corn on the cob, allow approximately:
☐ 5 minutes   ☐ 15 minutes
☐ 10 minutes   ☐ 30 minutes

55 What is the difference between fried onions and French fried onions?

56 What size onions would you select for braising?

57★ What is the price of onions?

58 ½kg (1lb) of fresh peas in the pod will yield approximately ..... portions.

59 ½kg (1 lb) of frozen peas will yield approximately ..... portions.

60 Which of the following would you use in preparing peas, French style?

☐ lettuce and button onions   ☐ mushrooms and button onions
☐ lettuce and mushrooms   ☐ mushrooms and garlic

61 A mixture of peas and carrots is known as .... style.

62 When preparing stuffed pimento, would you use red pimento or green pimento?

63★ What is the price of red pimento?

64 The base of the stuffing used for stuffed pimento is:

☐ breadcrumbs   ☐ mixed vegetables
☐ sausagemeat   ☐ rice

65 Salsify should be cooked in a blanc: true/false.

66★ What is the price of salsify?

67 To remove the skins from tomatoes plunge them into boiling water for approximately:

☐ 1–2 seconds   ☐ 5–6 seconds
☐ 3–4 seconds   ☐ 9–10 seconds

68 What ingredients are added to tomatoes to make tomato concassé?

69★ What is the current market price of English tomatoes?

70★ What is the current market price of imported tomatoes?

71 1 kg (2 lb) leeks prepared for braising will yield approximately:

☐ 1 portion   ☐ 3 portions
☐ 2 portions   ☐ 4 portions

72 When preparing pease pudding it is usual to use:

☐ frozen peas   ☐ split green peas
☐ tinned peas   ☐ split yellow peas

73 Is it more efficient to cook pease pudding:

☐ on top of the stove   ☐ in the oven

74 What ingredients in addition to peas would you add to pease pudding to improve the flavour?

75 Which of the following is used in a dish of mixed vegetables (macedoine de légumes)?

☐ swedes, turnips, haricot beans, peas
☐ swedes, turnips, mushrooms
☐ carrots, turnips, mushrooms
☐ carrots, turnips, peas and French beans

76

Peas + Lettuce + Button onions + Beurre manié =

77 Aubergine – Cucumber – Marrow – Courgette
Which is which?

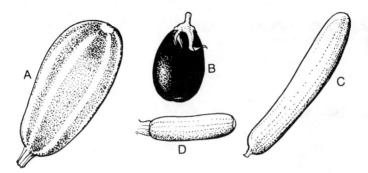

19
Potatoes

pages 354–357

1★ In what shapes or forms are prepared potatoes available?

2★ Approximately how many portions can be obtained from ½kg (1 lb) of old potatoes?

New potatoes?

3 Even-sized boiled potatoes will cook in approximately:
- ☐ 10 minutes
- ☐ 15 minutes
- ☐ 20 minutes
- ☐ 30 minutes

4 Parsley potatoes are cooked by:
- ☐ boiling
- ☐ roasting
- ☐ sautéing
- ☐ frying

5 Riced potatoes are a mixture of half potatoes half rice: true/false.

6 Why do we add butter or margarine and warm milk to mashed potatoes?

7 What ingredients can be added to mashed potatoes in order to make a variation?

8 What ingredients are added to dry mashed potato in order to make duchess potatoes?

9 Why do we dry-off duchess potatoes after piping, before brushing them with egg-wash?

10 Brioche potatoes are made from:

☐ mashed potatoes ☐ sauté potatoes
☐ duchess potatoes ☐ baked jacket potatoes

11* Why should croquette potatoes be passed through flour, egg and crumbs before being deep fried?

12 What is added to duchess potato to make marquis potatoes?

☐ onion ☐ cheese ☐ tomato

13 The best way to pre-cook potatoes for pommes sauté is:
☐ boil in jacket ☐ peel and boil
☐ steam in jacket ☐ peel, slice and steam

14 When preparing pommes lyonnaise, you should allow two parts onion to one part potatoes: true/false.

15 Game chips should be cooked in cool fat: true/false.

16 When giving chipped potatoes their 'first fry' the temperature of the fat should be:

☐ 100°C ☐ 140°C
☐ 120°C ☐ 165°C

17 After frying and before serving, chipped potatoes should be lightly seasoned with salt: true/false.

18 Which of the following are prepared from a baked jacket potato?

☐ pommes Macaire ☐ pommes marquise
☐ pommes bataille ☐ pommes fondantes

19 When preparing pommes boulangère (savoury potatoes) you should use two parts of potato to one part of onion: true/false.

20 How long does it take to cook four portions of pommes boulangère?

☐ 20 minutes ☐ 1 hour
☐ 45 minutes ☐ 1½ hours

21 Fondant potatoes are even-sized, brushed with butter or margarine and cooked in stock in the oven: true/false.

22 Which potato dish has bacon, onion, chopped parsley and white stock added during cooking?

☐ rissolées   ☐ mignonnette
☐ berrichonne   ☐ Anna

23 Roast potatoes should be cooked in a hot oven 230°–250°: true/false.

24 Both château potatoes and fondant potatoes are cooked in stock in the oven: true/false.

25 Noisette potatoes are turned with a small kitchen knife: true/false.

26 Parisienne potatoes should be finished by rolling in a little meat glaze: true/false.

27 Diced potatoes, button onions, lardons, cooked in stock are known as:

☐ pommes au lard   ☐ Parmentier
☐ Delmonico   ☐ bataille

28 Delmonico potatoes are cooked in white stock: true/false.

29 There is only one efficient method of plain boiling new potatoes: true/false.

30 Parmentier potatoes should be deep fried: true/false.

31 Pommes Anna like pommes boulangère should contain a proportion of finely sliced onion: true/false.

32 Name two potatoes cut in each shape.

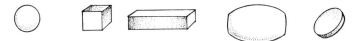

33 Show the correct letter against the appropriate name.

Pont-neuf
Frite
Paille
Gaufrette
Bataille

20
Pastry

pages 368–374

1 What pastry would you use for Cornish pasties and fruit pies?

☐ puff   ☐ flaky

☐ rough puff   ☐ short

2 The usual proportion of fat to flour for short pastry is:

☐ 1 part fat to 1 part flour

☐ 1 part fat to 2 parts flour

☐ 1 part fat to 3 parts flour

☐ 1 part fat to 4 parts flour

3 When being mixed, short pastry should be handled firmly and well kneaded: true/false.

4 Give one possible reason for each of the following faults in short pastry:

1 hard

2 soft-crumbly

3 blistered

4 soggy

5 shrunken

5 When making puff pastry would you use strong flour or soft flour?

6 The usual proportion of fat to flour for puff pastry is:

☐ 1 part fat to 1 part flour

☐ 1 part fat to 2 parts flour

☐ 1 part fat to 3 parts flour

☐ 1 part fat to 4 parts flour

7★ Why is it essential to rest the paste between the various stages of making puff pastry?

8★ What are the current market prices of:

flour	margarine
lard	cooking fat
butter	

9 What causes the lift or lightness in puff pastry?

10 Why is an acid such as lemon juice added when making puff pastry?

11 Give one reason for each of the following faults in puff pastry:

not flaky	shrunken
fat oozes out	soggy
hard	uneven rise

12 The usual proportion of fat to flour for rough puff pastry is:

- ☐ 1 part fat to 1 part flour
- ☐ 1 part fat to 2 parts flour
- ☐ 3 parts fat to 4 parts flour
- ☐ 3 parts fat to 5 parts flour

13 It is best to use sugar paste immediately after it has been made: true/false.

14★ What are the prices of:

castor sugar	loaf sugar
granulated sugar	icing sugar

15 Which paste would you use for flans and fruit tartlets?

☐ short   ☐ rough puff   ☐ sugar

16 Baking powder is used in making suet paste? True/false.

17 The usual proportion of suet to flour in suet paste is:

☐ 1 part suet to 1 part flour
☐ 1 part suet to 2 parts flour
☐ 1 part suet to 3 parts flour
☐ 1 part suet to 4 parts flour

18 Give one reason for each of the following faults in suet paste:

heavy-soggy
tough
lumps of suet

19 What is hot water paste used for?

20 At what temperature should hot water paste be used?

☐ hot ☐ cold ☐ warm

21 The approximate number of eggs per ½ litre (1 pint) of choux paste is:

☐ 4 ☐ 12
☐ 8 ☐ 16

22★ What is the current price of eggs?

23 Name three items prepared from choux paste:

1 2 3

24 Choux paste should be of a dropping consistency: true/false.

25 Give one reason for each of the following faults in choux paste:

greasy and heavy

soft – not aerated

26 How many scones would you expect to make from a mixture using 200g (½lb) flour base?

27 What would you add to a basic scone mixture to make fruit scones?

☐ currants ☐ angelica and cherries
☐ raisins ☐ sultanas

28 Give four variations to basic small cake mixture.

1   2

3   4

29 Give one reason for each of the following faults in sponges:

close texture   sunken

holey   white spots on surface

30 A genoese sponge contains butter: true/false.

31 The proportion of fat to flour in genoese is:

☐ 1 part fat to 1 part flour
☐ 1 part fat to 2 parts flour
☐ 1 part fat to 3 parts flour
☐ 1 part fat to 4 parts flour

32 What ingredient is added to the basic mixture for genoese in order to make chocolate genoese?

33 What should be the flavour of gâteau moka?

34 Give one reason for each of the following faults in yeast dough:

close texture
uneven texture
coarse texture
wrinkled
sour
broken crust
white spots on crust

35 Flour for making bread and rolls should be a strong flour and should be warmed: true/false.

36 What happens when you prove a yeast dough?

37 What two extra ingredients are added to a basic dough in order to make bun dough?

1   2

38★ What is the price of yeast?

39 Give three examples of goods made from bun dough.

1   2   3

40 Doughnuts should be fried in:

☐ cool fat   ☐ hot fat
☐ moderately hot fat   ☐ very hot fat

41 Savarin paste contains yeast: true/false.

42 What two ingredients are added to savarin paste in order to make rum babas?

43 Crème Chantilly is:

☐ plain single cream
☐ half whipped double cream
☐ whipped cream sweetened and flavoured with vanilla
☐ a special type of pastry cream

44 What ingredients would you use in preparing a syrup for soaking babas?

45 Which of the following is the odd one out and why?

☐ baba   ☐ meringue
☐ savarin   ☐ marignan

46 Name six fruits or combination of fruits suitable for making into a fruit pie.

1   2   3

4   5   6

47 Which ingredient is missing from the following list for the filling for a treacle tart?

1 syrup or treacle   2 lemon juice
3 water   4

48 Baked apple dumplings are usually made with:

☐ rough puff paste   ☐ short paste
☐ sugar paste   ☐ puff paste

49★ What is the price of cooking apples?

50 What two ingredients would you put into the centre of an apple before covering it with pastry for a baked apple dumpling?

1   2

51 Which of the following would you add to Dutch apple tart?

☐ currants   ☐ sultanas
☐ raisins   ☐ dates

52 An apple flan should be finished with:

☐ red glaze   ☐ icing sugar
☐ yellow jelly   ☐ apricot glaze

53 Should cherries in a cherry flan be stoned? Yes/no.

54 Fruit flans should be cooked in:

☐ cool oven   ☐ moderately hot oven
☐ hot oven   ☐ fierce oven

55 What may be placed as a layer on the base of a rhubarb flan?

56★ What is the price of rhubarb?

57 Name three types of fruit flan for which you would cook the flan case blind.

1   2   3

58 Would you cook the flan case 'blind' for a banana flan? Yes/no.

59★ What is the price of bananas?

60 Is it usual to put a layer on the base of a banana flan? Yes/no. If so, what would you use?

61 What is the difference between a strawberry tartlet and a strawberry barquette?

62★ What is the price of fresh strawberries in season?

63★ What is the price of frozen strawberries?

64 What is the distinctive flavouring in the filling of bakewell tart?

65 What jam should be used in the base of a bakewell tart?

☐ apricot   ☐ raspberry
☐ strawberry   ☐ red plum

66 What is the main filling in a lemon meringue pie?

67★ What is the price of a dozen lemons?

68 What item could be made from the following ingredients?

100g (4oz) butter or margarine   100g (4oz) castor sugar
2 eggs   1 lemon

69 What is the difference between a jam turnover and a jam puff?

70 Which paste would you use for cream horns?

☐ short paste   ☐ flaky paste
☐ sugar paste   ☐ puff paste

71 Would you place a little jam in the bottom of a cream horn after cooking and before filling with cream? Yes/no.

72 Cream horns should be baked in:

☐ hot oven   ☐ cool oven
☐ moderately hot oven   ☐ very hot oven

73 What is the reason for sprinkling some puff pastry goods with icing sugar and returning them to a hot oven at the last stage of cooking?

74 What is the English for mille-feuilles?

75★ What is the literal translation of mille-feuilles?

76 What is the traditional filling for mille-feuilles?

77★ Which of the traditional fillings for a mille-feuilles is sometimes varied because of popular taste?

78 What is the term given to the traditional decorative finish for a mille-feuilles?

79 Which of the following would be the odd one out as a filling for jalousie?

☐ mincemeat ☐ jam
☐ frangipane ☐ apple

80 Which filling would you use for a gâteau pithivier?

☐ marzipan ☐ cooked rice
☐ mincemeat ☐ frangipane

81 To make palmiers it is essential to use good puff pastry: true/false.

82 How can you make two palmiers into a tea pastry?

83 Suggest two sauces suitable for serving with mince pies.

1   2

84 How many bouchées should be obtained from puff pastry using 200g (½lb) flour?

85 Bouchées should be cooked on greased, dampened baking sheets: true/false.

86 What is the name given to large bouchées?

87 What variation in flavour in addition to chocolate is used for éclairs?

88 What happens to the fondant glaze on éclairs if it is overheated?

89 What ingredient may be sprinkled on cream buns before they are baked?

90 How would you finish cream buns before service?

91 What are profiteroles?

92 In how many sizes may profiteroles be made, and for what purpose?

93 When serving profiteroles filled with cream as a sweet, which sauce would you offer?

☐ jam   ☐ vanilla
☐ raspberry   ☐ chocolate

94 What are pieces of choux paste the size of a walnut cooked in deep fat called?

95 Suggest three fruits or combination of fruits suitable for steamed fruit suet pudding.

1   2   3

96 What is the approximate cooking time for a steamed fruit pudding?

☐ 1 hour   ☐ 2½ hours
☐ 1½ hours   ☐ 3 hours

97 Give the basic quantities of ingredients for six portions steamed sponge pudding.

castor sugar   margarine

eggs   flour

baking powder   milk

98 Suggest six variations for a steamed sponge pudding together with a sauce that you would offer with each:

1

2

3

4

5

6

99 Why is a soufflé pudding so called?

100 Soufflé pudding should be cooked in a bain-marie in a hot oven: true/false.

101 What is the dominant flavour of soufflé milanaise?

102 What is the top layer on queen of puddings?

☐ breadcrumbs   ☐ meringue
☐ baked custard   ☐ thin sheet of puff pastry

103 What thickness would you cut apple rings for apple fritters?

☐ ½ cm (¼ in)   ☐ 1½ cm (¾ in)
☐ 1 cm (½ in)   ☐ 2 cm (1 in)

104 In a fairly hot fat, apple fritters require approximately:

☐ 2 minutes on each side   ☐ 4 minutes on each side
☐ 3 minutes on each side   ☐ 5 minutes on each side

105 What sauce would you offer with apple fritters?

☐ custard   ☐ syrup
☐ apricot   ☐ orange

106 What fruits are suitable for serving as fritters?

107 Complete this list of quantities of ingredients for pancake batter:

100 g flour (4 oz)   egg
milk   melted butter or margarine
pinch of salt

108 Suggest three ways of serving pancakes

1   2   3

109 What is a pomme bonne femme?

110 Suggest a suitable stuffing for a baked apple.

111 List six fresh fruits suitable for fruit salad.

1   2   3

4   5   6

112 What ingredient added to milk causes it to coagulate or clot?

113 What is the name of the sweet made by the process in question 112 and what other ingredients should be added?

114 Which spice is generally used to sprinkle on junket?
- ☐ clove
- ☐ cinnamon
- ☐ nutmeg
- ☐ ginger

115 Suggest four suitable fruits for making fruit fool.

1

2

3

4

116 Suggest four suitable fruits for including in a fruit trifle.

1

2

3

4

117 How much sugar is needed for meringue using four egg whites?

118 As the aim when cooking meringues is to cook them without colouring they should be cooked in the slowest oven possible: true/false.

119 Name four important points to be observed when whipping egg whites.

1

2

3

4

120 Why do egg whites increase in volume when whipped?

121 How would you serve meringue chantilly?

122 What is a vacherin?
- ☐ two meringues joined by a ball of ice cream
- ☐ two meringues joined by whipped cream
- ☐ a special mould for shaping meringue
- ☐ a round case of meringue shell

123 What is the name of the sweet with a base of sponge, a layer of ice cream and a coating of meringue, browned in the oven?

124 Translate compôte des fruits.

125 What is the correct finish for a jam omelet?

126 Name four types of simple milk puddings

1   2

3   4

127 What is a fruit condé?

128 Name four fruits suitable for preparing as a condé.

1   2

3   4

129 What glaze is used to finish a condé?

130★ What is the price of rice?

131 What proportion of eggs to milk is required for a baked egg custard?

☐ 4 size 3 eggs 1 litre (2 pints) milk
☑ 6 size 3 eggs 1 litre (2 pints) milk
☐ 8 size 3 eggs 1 litre (2 pints) milk
☐ 10 size 3 eggs 1 litre (2 pints) milk

132 What fruit would you use in a bread and butter pudding?

☐ dates   ☑ sultanas
☐ figs   ☐ apricots

133 It is not necessary to cook a bread and butter pudding in a bain-marie provided the oven is cool enough: true/false.

134 What sweet can be made from stale bread?

135 What sweet with an egg custard base is made using diced sponge and fruit?

136 What name is given to the sweet in question 135 when served cold?

137 Add the quantities to this list of ingredients for cream caramel.

milk ½ litre (1 pint)
sugar
eggs
vanilla

caramel
sugar
water

138 Cream caramels should be cooked in a bain-marie in:

☐ a hot oven
☐ a fierce oven
☐ a cool oven
☑ a moderately hot oven

139★ What is bavarois?

140 Suggest six varieties of bavarois.

1   2   3

4   5   6

141 A charlotte russe is a variation of a basic bavarois recipe: true/false.

142 What is pastry cream?

☐ whipped sweetened cream for filling pastries
☐ a basic pastry preparation of thick custard
☐ bavarois mixture in pastry cases
☐ mock cream used as a substitute for fresh cream

143 Which of the following ice creams is prepared as a water ice?

☐ vanilla ☐ lemon
☐ chocolate ☐ coffee

144 The correct ice cream used for pear Belle Hélène is:
☐ vanilla ☐ strawberry
☐ chocolate ☐ coffee

145 What is a sabayon sauce?

146 Suggest a suitable hot sweet for serving accompanied by a sauce sabayon.

147 What is a zabaglione?

pages 438–443

148 Which is:

Eclair
Cream bun
Profiterole

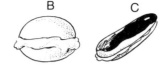

The basic mixture used for above items is:

149 What are the two basic categories of petit fours?

1   2

150 List four examples of petit fours in each of the two categories mentioned in question 149.

Category 1	*Category 2*
a	a
b	b
c	c
d	d

151 What type of sugar is used in making langues de chat?

☐ brown   ☐ granulated
☐ castor   ☐ icing

152 What can be used to shape cornets after they are cooked?

153 What is praline?

154 How is praline made?

155 What is praline used for?

156 Name the eight stages of cooking sugar in order:

1 small thread	5
2	6
3	7
4	8 caramel

157 Re-arrange names on to correct items

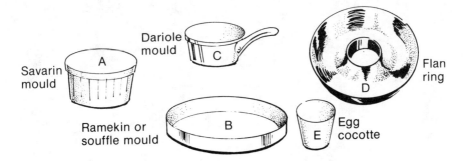

158 Which piece of equipment would be used for:

Mixing dough

Whisking egg whites

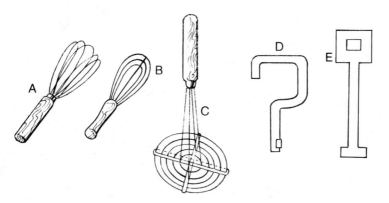

159 How would you divide these gâteaux into even-sized pieces?

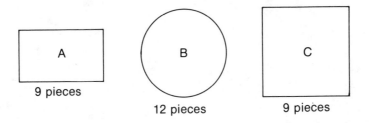

9 pieces

12 pieces

9 pieces

160   Which is the odd one out?   Why?

A

Vol-au-vent

B

Bouchée

C

Mille-feuille

D

Fruit tartlet

21
Savouries

pages 444–448

1 What is the difference between Angels on horseback and Devils on horseback?

2 With what are prunes stuffed in the preparation for Devils on horseback?

3★ Devilled kidneys are only suitable for a luncheon dish: true/false.

4 Which mushrooms would you select for mushrooms on toast?

☐ button   ☐ open

5★ What is the current market price for:

button mushrooms   open mushrooms

6 Suggest two ways of serving curried shrimps or prawns as a savoury.

1   2

7★ What are the prices of prepared shrimps and prepared prawns?

8 What are the ingredients of a croque monsieur?

☐ ham, cheese, toast   ☐ ham, mushroom, toast
☐ bacon, cheese, toast   ☐ bacon, mushroom, toast

9 The chief ingredient in Derby toast is:

☐ ham   ☐ shrimp
☐ mushroom   ☐ prawns

10 Derby toast is topped with:

☐ mushroom   ☐ grated cheese
☐ pickled walnut   ☐ slice of tomato

11 Canapé Yarmouth consists of which fish on toast?

☐ smoked haddock ☐ kipper
☐ bloater ☐ salmon

12★ What price are:

smoked haddock   bloater

kipper   smoked salmon

13 When preparing soft roes on toast, the roes need not be floured: true/false.

14★ What is the price of soft roes?

15 How would you cook soft roes?

☐ grilling ☐ poaching ☐ boiling
☐ baking ☐ frying

16 What has Canapé Diane in common with Angels on horseback and Devils on horseback?

17 Scotch woodcock is:

☐ a game bird from Scotland
☐ a colloquial term for tripe as prepared in Glasgow
☐ scrambled eggs on toast garnished with anchovies and capers
☐ a game pâté first produced in Balmoral

18 What type of bacon would you use for haddock and bacon savouries?

☐ back ☐ streaky
☐ gammon ☐ collar

19 Suggest two variations that can be made to a basic creamed haddock on toast.

1   2

20 The ingredients for Canapé Nina are:
☐ mushroom, walnut, tomato ☐ mushroom, bacon, cheese
☐ mushroom, walnut, stoned ☐ mushroom, ham, walnut
  olive

21 Which cheese would you use for Welsh rarebit?

☐ Stilton ☐ Wensleydale
☐ Caerphilly ☐ Cheddar

22 Suggest four seasonings or flavourings that can be used when making Welsh rarebit.

1   2

3   4

23 A buck rarebit is a Welsh rarebit with the addition of:

☐ bacon ☐ ham
☐ mushroom ☐ poached egg

24 What is the base of a cheese soufflé mixture?

25 When making cheese soufflé, how many egg whites would you add to the following mixture?

butter 25g (1oz)   flour 15g (¾oz)
milk 125 ml (¼ pint)   egg yolks 3
egg whites   grated cheese 50g (2 oz)
salt   cayenne

26 Approximately how long would the mixture in question 25 take to cook in a hot oven?

☐ 5 minutes ☐ 10–12 minutes
☐ 15–20 minutes ☐ 25–30 minutes

27 When a soufflé is cooked, if not required immediately it should be stood in a bain-marie and kept in the top of a hot plate: true/false.

28 What two ingredients are added to puff pastry in order to make cheese straws?

1   2

29 Translate beignets de fromage.

30 Translate quiche lorraine.

31 Suggest an interesting filling for a savoury flan.

pages 456, 445

32   What pastry would you use for a savoury flan?

33   Which item would be used in angels on horseback?

Egg

Sprat

Oyster

Prunes

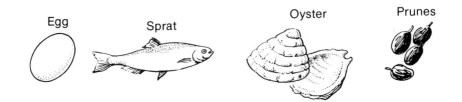

Multiple Choice Questions

1 'Mise en place' means:

    ☐ **a** clearing up afterwards   ☐ **c** replacing items used
    ☐ **b** preparing in advance   ☐ **d** returning food to store

2 Which joint of beef is most suitable for salting?

    ☐ **a** shin   ☐ **c** thick flank
    ☐ **b** silverside   ☐ **d** sirloin

3 To boil rice allow approximately:

    ☐ **a** 5 minutes   ☐ **c** 30 minutes
    ☐ **b** 15 minutes   ☐ **d** 1 hour

4 Which of the following is prepared from baked jacket potatoes?

    ☐ **a** fondant potatoes   ☐ **c** duchess potatoes
    ☐ **b** macaire potatoes   ☐ **d** croquette potatoes

5 A mandolin is used for:

    ☐ **a** dicing   ☐ **c** slicing
    ☐ **b** chopping   ☐ **d** mincing

6 Espagnole is the basic sauce used for:

    ☐ **a** roast gravy   ☐ **c** piquant sauce
    ☐ **b** tomato sauce   ☐ **d** suprême sauce

7 A tronçon is:

    ☐ **a** a fillet of fish   ☐ **c** steak from a round fish
    ☐ **b** a slice of flat fish on the bone   ☐ **d** a cutlet of fish

8 What is jus lié?

    ☐ **a** thin gravy   ☐ **c** thickened gravy
    ☐ **b** meat juice   ☐ **d** brown sauce

9 An egg custard can curdle during cooking because:

☐ **a** too many eggs have been used
☐ **b** inaccurate amount of sugar used
☐ **c** too great a degree of heat
☐ **d** inferior quality eggs used

10 In which of the following is sieved potato used?

☐ **a** pommes château
☐ **b** pommes lyonnaise
☐ **c** pommes duchesse
☐ **d** pommes fondantes

11 Approximately how many bouchées should ½ kg (1 lb) puff paste yield?

☐ **a** 12
☐ **b** 24
☐ **c** 36
☐ **d** 48

12 After use, an omelet pan is cleaned by:

☐ **a** plunging into hot water
☐ **b** cleaning with steel wool
☐ **c** rubbing with an abrasive powder
☐ **d** wiping with a clean cloth

13 Apple pie is usually covered with:

☐ **a** puff pastry
☐ **b** crumble
☐ **c** short pastry
☐ **d** flaky pastry

14 The term meunière means:

☐ **a** shallow fried
☐ **b** grilled
☐ **c** deep fried
☐ **d** crumbed and fried

15 Which of the following is a basic sauce?

☐ **a** béchamel
☐ **b** anchovy
☐ **c** suprême
☐ **d** chaud-froid

16 Chicken Maryland is:

☐ **a** boiled
☐ **b** fried
☐ **c** braised
☐ **d** roasted

17 Which of the following is an oily fish?

☐ **a** herring
☐ **b** halibut
☐ **c** hake
☐ **d** haddock

18 Fish stock should simmer for:

☐ **a** 20 minutes   ☐ **c** 60 minutes
☐ **b** 40 minutes   ☐ **d** 90 minutes

19 Beef olives should be cooked by:

☐ **a** boiling   ☐ **c** frying
☐ **b** braising   ☐ **d** steaming

20 Junket is made from:

☐ **a** sweet milk and gelatine   ☐ **c** sweet milk and riceflour
☐ **b** sweet milk and cornflour   ☐ **d** sweet milk and rennet

21 To produce 4½ litres (1 gallon) of beef stock use:

☐ **a** 400 g (1lb) of bones   ☐ **c** 5 kg (10lb) of bones
☐ **b** 2 kg (4lb) of bones   ☐ **d** 6 kg (12lb) of bones

22 Which sauce is served with shallow fried breadcrumbed lamb cutlets?

☐ **a** chasseur   ☐ **c** reform
☐ **b** lyonnaise   ☐ **d** bercy

23 Saignant is a term meaning:

☐ **a** well done   ☐ **c** medium rare
☐ **b** underdone   ☐ **d** slowly charred

24 Choucroûte is made with:

☐ **a** cauliflower   ☐ **c** sea-kale
☐ **b** kale   ☐ **d** cabbage

25 A noisette is cut from which joint of lamb?

☐ **a** shoulder   ☐ **c** loin
☐ **b** leg   ☐ **d** neck

26 A salamander is used for:

☐ **a** grilling   ☐ **c** roasting
☐ **b** boiling   ☐ **d** steaming

27 The proportion of sugar to whites of egg for meringue is:

☐ **a** 1 white to 50 g (2oz) sugar   ☐ **c** 1 white to 100 g (4oz) sugar
☐ **b** 1 white to 75 g (3oz) sugar   ☐ **d** 1 white to 125 g (5oz) sugar

28 Osso buco is made with:

    ☐ **a** shoulder of lamb   ☐ **c** knuckle of lamb
    ☐ **b** shoulder of veal   ☐ **d** knuckle of veal

29 A salmis is:

    ☐ **a** lamb stew   ☐ **c** game stew
    ☐ **b** veal stew   ☐ **d** beef stew

30 Condé is made using:

    ☐ **a** semolina   ☐ **c** sago
    ☐ **b** rice   ☐ **d** tapioca

31 The accompaniments to roast grouse are:

    ☐ **a** watercress, roast gravy, game chips, chipolata, bacon
    ☐ **b** watercress, bread sauce, breadcrumbs, chipolata, ham
    ☐ **c** watercress, roast gravy, bread sauce, game chips, bacon
    ☐ **d** watercress, roast gravy, bread sauce, game chips, breadcrumbs

32 Prunes are used in:

    ☐ **a** devils on horseback   ☐ **c** Welsh rarebit
    ☐ **b** Scotch woodcock   ☐ **d** canapé Diane

33 A chicken cut resembling a toad is called:

    ☐ **a** spatchcock   ☐ **c** grenouille
    ☐ **b** capilotade   ☐ **d** ballottine

34 A Gâteau Pithivier in addition to puff pastry has:

    ☐ **a** apricot jam, marzipan and icing sugar
    ☐ **b** royal icing, almond paste and apricot jam
    ☐ **c** apricot jam, frangipane and icing sugar
    ☐ **d** apricot jam, royal icing and marzipan

35 Grated cheese and cream with macaire potatoes is called:

    ☐ **a** pommes Delmonico   ☐ **c** pommes dauphine
    ☐ **b** pommes Byron   ☐ **d** pommes marquise

36 Poulet à la king contains:

    ☐ **a** beef, demi-glace and   ☐ **c** lamb, jus-lié and rice
    red wine
    ☐ **b** chicken, chicken velouté and ☐ **d** veal, mushrooms and
    sherry   tomato sauce

37 Gelatine is added to bavarois:

   ☐ **a** after adding the cream   ☐ **c** when the custard is cold
   ☐ **b** when heating the milk   ☐ **d** when the custard is hot

38 A fish dish containing chopped parsley, chopped shallots, sliced mushrooms, mushrooms, and diced tomato is called:

   ☐ **a** Bréval   ☐ **c** bonne femme
   ☐ **b** Bercy   ☐ **d** berrichonne

39 As an accompaniment to turtle soup, which of the following would be served?

   ☐ **a** fleurons   ☐ **c** canapés
   ☐ **c** croûtons   ☐ **d** cheese straws

40 Which dish would be served as a sweet?
   ☐ **a** pomme en robe de chambre   ☐ **c** pomme au four
   ☐ **b** pomme en cage   ☐ **d** pomme à la neige

Mixed Questions

1 Name two typical British dishes using stewing lamb

a   b

2 Which cuts from the carcass of lamb could be used for grilling?
a   b   c

3 The term for vegetables cut into thin strips is?

4 A bouquet garni usually consists of:

  ☐ **a** onions, carrots, celery, leek ☐ **c** parsley, bayleaf, thyme, celery

  ☐ **b** sage, onion, parsley, leek ☐ **d** celery, leek, bayleaf, rosemary

5 The approximate imperial equivalent of 1 litre is

6 The culinary term to 'sweat' means?

7 What is the name of the small item of equipment on which kebabs are pierced?

8 Name three British tea pastries

a   b   c

9 Name three French tea pastries

a   b   c

10 List the points to be considered when correcting a cream soup

1   2

3   4

5

11 Name four herbs used in cooking

1   2

3   4

12 It is better to overseason than underseason: true/false.

13 The 'Guide to Modern Cookery' was written by

14 What is the translation of topinambours?

☐ **a** Jersey potatoes   ☐ **c** Brussels sprouts
☐ **b** Jerusalem artichokes   ☐ **d** French artichokes

15 Melon is usually served as a.. course.

16 List four vegetables suitable for braising.

1   2

3   4

17 Suggest an interesting selection of eight suitable dishes for a sweet trolley.

1   5

2   6

3   7

4   8

18 Fried potatoes when served are covered with a lid: true/false.

19 Which of the following is the odd one out and why? Cream horns, Eccles cakes, jam tarts, cream slice.

20 Give a brief description of:

a Welsh rarebit

b Scotch woodcock

c Irish stew

21 Place labels in correct order

Croquette

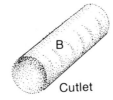

Cutlet

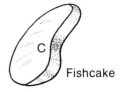

Fishcake

Humorous Questions

1   When is a mushroom not a mushroom?

2   When is a spider welcome in the kitchen?

3   Is a cock-a-leekie an ardent Welsh football fan?

4   Would you expect movement in a still-room?

5   Would you be entitled to grumble on the 12th August?

6   Does a craving for fruit make you a fruit fool?

7   Would you serve apple sauce and sage and onion stuffing with Bombay Duck?

8   Is a Bath Chap a Somerset farmer's boy?

9   Is a papillotte an ancient Egyptian scroll?

10   Why are dead man's fingers dangerous?

11   Is it true that cat's tongues are served to customers?

12   What could you put in a puff of wind?

13   Which have culinary connections: a bullet, a shell, a cannon, a bomb, a rocket?

14   When did the welsh rarebit become a gentleman rarebit?

15   What is served in a dressing gown?

16   Would you serve game chips and gravy with Scotch woodcock?

17   Are culinary capers when chefs dance in the kitchen?

18   Why was the vegetable cook interested in the ladies' fingers?

19   When did you prove the dough was OK?

20   Where will the Beauty of Bath, Queen Claude, Royal Sovereign and the Doyenne du Comice meet together?

Answers

(To Multiple Choice, Mixed, Humorous and Diagram Questions)

Multiple Choice Answers

1 b 2 b 3 b 4 b 5 c 6 c 7 b 8 c 9 c 10 c 11 b 12 d 13 c 14 a 15 a
16 b 17 a 18 a 19 b 20 d 21 b 22 c 23 b 24 d 25 c 26 a 27 a 28 d
29 c 30 b 31 d 32 a 33 a 34 c 35 b 36 b 37 d 38 a 39 d 40 b

Mixed Questions – Suggested answers (in some cases there are alternative answers).

1 Lancashire hot pot, Irish stew.
2 Cutlet, loin chop, chump chop.
3 Julienne.
4 c.
5 1 quart.
6 To cook in fat under a lid without colour.
7 Skewer or brochette.
8 Maids of honour, macaroons, queen cake.
9 Eclairs, mille feuilles, fruit tartlet.
10 Seasoning, consistency, colour, temperature, texture.
11 Sage, parsley, thyme, bayleaf
12 False.
13 Escoffier.
14 b.
15 First.
16 Celery, cabbage, onion, leeks.
17 Fruit salad, trifle, flan, gâteau, profiteroles, creme caramel, pithiviers, charlotte russe.
18 False.
19 Jam tarts (short paste).
20 **a** Cheese mixture on toast, **b** Scrambled eggs on toast with capers and anchovies, **c** White stew of lamb thickened with potato and onion.
21 A. Fish cakes. B. Croquette. C. Cutlet.

Humorous Questions – Answers

1 When it is a small wooden utensil for pushing food through a sieve.
2 When it is a wire utensil used for lifting out solid items.
3 No, it is a soup which includes chicken and leek.

122

4 Yes, because staff serve beverages from this room.
5 No, this is the date when 'grouse' shooting commences.
6 Hardly – a fruit fool is a mixture of sieved fruit and cream or custard.
7 No, it is a dried fish – served with curry.
8 No, it is the pig's cheek which has been cured.
9 No, it is a method of cooking by sealing in greaseproof paper or foil.
10 They are part of the crab which may contain poison.
11 Yes they are a flat tongue-shaped biscuit – langue de chat.
12 Chicken, prawns etc., it is a vol-au-vent.
13 A shell – e.g. meringue. A bomb – ice cream.
14 When it has a poached egg on top – buck rarebit.
15 A steamed potato in its jacket (pomme en robe de chambre).
16 No, a scotch woodcock is a savoury.
17 Not likely, culinary capers are pickled flower buds of the caper plant.
18 Because they are a type of vegetable (okra).
19 When it had risen.
20 In a fruit salad or in a fruit basket.

Diagram Questions – Answers

P.7 **15** A Boiling   B Stewing, boiling, frying etc.   C Steaming
D Grilling

P.13 **68** A. steaming   B. grilling   C. boiling   D. frying   E. roasting
F. braising
69 Deep frying

P.18 **43** 2   4   3   1
44 1) brunoise   2) macédoine   3) jardinière   4) julienne   5) paysanne

P.29 **28** Look at your diagram and check that colours, textures and main
ingredients are arranged in a varied and pleasing manner.

P.30 **34** A. ravier   B. marmite   C. cocotte

P.31 **49** Waldorf

P.40 **19** C. Omelet   B. Egg in cocotte   A. Oeuf sur le plat

P.44 **30** 1. vermicelli 2. macaroni   3. spaghetti   4. pâte d'italie
5. ravioli   6. canneloni
31 1.D   2.B   3.A   4.C

P.51 **69** A. tronçon B. filet C. suprême D. darne E. paupiette

P.56 **49** A. Cutlet B. Chop

P.56 **50** A. Cutlets – best end   B. chops – loin

P.62 **50** oysters **51** C. **52** suet   puff   short
                                    steak & kidney   chicken   mutton

P.66 **41** A

P.69 **24** A

P.72 **22** A. Gammon   B. Ham

P.80 **78** A. Jugged Hare   B. Scotch Woodcock   C. Cream Slice
          Civet de Lièvre   Mille-Feuilles

P.81 **79** A. Jugged Hare   B. Thick soup C. Canapés   D. Roast game
     80 A. Trussing   B. Larding   C. Opening Oysters

P.88 **76** Petits pois à la Française

P.89 **77** A. Marrow   B. Aubergine   C. Cucumber
          D. Courgette

P.92 **32** Parisienne Bataille   Frites   Château   Chips
          Noisette   Parmentier Allumettes Fondantes Sautées

33 E   C   D   B   A

P.106 **148** Eclair C   Cream bun B   Profiterole A   Choux paste

P.107 **157** A. Ramekin or Soufflé mould B. Flan ring   C. Egg cocotte
            D. Savarin mould   E. Dariole mould
      158 D   A

159

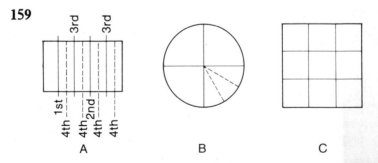

A   B   C

P.108 **160** Fruit tartlet, made with short or sugar paste. The other three
            are made with puff paste.
P.112 **33** Oysters